THE ULTIMATE BOOK OF

CHILI & SPICE

THE ULTIMATE BOOK OF

CHILI & SPICE

100 RECIPES TO HEAT UP
& SPICE UP YOUR LIFE

This edition published by Cottage Door Press, LLC, in 2020.
First published 2017 by Parragon Books, Ltd.

Copyright © 2020 Cottage Door Press, LLC
5005 Newport Drive, Rolling Meadows, Illinois 60008

The cover shows (clockwise from top left): Sticky Bourbon Chicken
Wings (28); Chimichurri Sweltering Sauce (80); Eggplant Paprika Salad (57);
Tabbouleh-Stuffed Jalapeños (12); Spiced Turkey Stew with Whole Grain
Couscous (157); Mexican Turkey Burgers, shown with bell peppers (154);
Thai Green Chicken Curry & Udon Noodles (146).

ISBN: 978-1-68052-870-1

Printed in China

Love Food™ is an imprint of Cottage Door Press, LLC.
Parragon Books® and the Parragon® logo are registered trademarks
of Cottage Door Press, LLC.

NOTES FOR THE READER

This book uses standard kitchen measuring spoons and cups. All spoon and
cup measurements are level unless otherwise indicated. Unless otherwise
stated, milk is assumed to be whole, eggs are large, individual vegetables
are medium, and pepper is freshly ground black pepper. Unless otherwise
stated, all root vegetables should be peeled prior to using. People with nut
allergies should be aware that some of the prepared ingredients used in the
recipes in this book may contain nuts.

Garnishes, decorations, and serving suggestions are all optional and not
necessarily included in the recipe ingredients or method. The times given
are only an approximate guide. Preparation times differ according to the
techniques used by different people and the cooking times may also vary
from those given. Optional ingredients, variations, or serving suggestions
have not been included in the time calculations.

Take care when preparing chilies. The fiery heat comes from the chemical
compound capsaicin, located in the white pithy inner core or rib of the
chili. Capsaicin can aggravate skin and eyes, so always wash your hands
thoroughly after handling chilies. If your skin is sensitive, wear plastic
gloves. Never touch your eyes or mouth after handling chilies without
thoroughly washing your hands first with soap and water.

CONTENTS

CHILIES & SPICES
A CULINARY JOURNEY

If you're tired of preparing the same predictable meals and are craving something with a little more oomph, then look no further. *Chili & Spice* features 101 sizzling recipes from around the globe to help jazz up your dishes—warming appetizers, snacks and sides; fiery vegetarian, meat, and fish main courses; and tantalizing sweet treats.

SPICES

In ancient times, spices were used to prevent ingredients from spoiling and to disguise food with strong odors and unpleasant flavors. As they became popular for their aromatic flavors, spices were integrated into everyday cuisine, with countries and regions developing their own unique signature dishes based on available indigenous spices. Over time, people discovered the remarkable medicinal properties of specific spices.

Nowadays, we may not give much thought to our ubiquitous, affordable spices as we sprinkle them liberally over ingredients, but they have an incredible history. Once the world's biggest and most dominant industry, the spice trade produced great wealth for many nations. Spices were such precious commodities that nutmeg and pepper were worth more than gold.

The spice trade began with camel caravans in the Middle East some 4,000 years ago. Arabic spice traders spun elaborate myths about how hard the spices were to come by, thereby adding to their allure and driving up prices. The Silk Road connecting Asia with North Africa and Europe played a vital role in building mighty civilizations and empires, such as those of China, India, Egypt, Persia, Arabia, and Rome.

For centuries, Middle Eastern and North African traders monopolized the spice trade, becoming increasingly wealthy and powerful, and forcing European merchants to pay excessively high prices. By the 1400s, even the nobility struggled to pay for aromatic luxuries, so explorers were dispatched overseas in search of alternative trade routes.

First to cross the Atlantic Ocean was the Italian explorer Christopher Columbus, who accidentally stumbled across the Americas in 1492 while looking for precious black pepper and a more direct route to India. He discovered new fruit and vegetables, including corn, potatoes, pumpkins, pineapple, avocados, and papayas, and, perhaps most notably, the much-loved chili pepper.

In 1497, Portuguese explorer Vasco de Gama became the first to sail directly from Africa to India. His sea route around Africa opened up a trade between Europe and Asia, and it resulted in a Portuguese dominance of the spice trade that endured for centuries.

As spice cultivation began to spread around the world, availability became more widespread and prices fell. Once valuable spices, such as pepper, cinnamon, and nutmeg, are no longer the precious products they once were, but they are just as popular today, still cherished for their vibrant colors, pungent flavors, and enticing aromas.

CHILIES

Chili peppers are the pods of perennial, woody-stemmed shrubs that belong to the *Capsicum* genus. They originate from Central America, where archaeologists have found traces of their consumption by humans dating back to 7500 BCE. Chilies have been used as a primary ingredient in Mexican cooking for hundreds of years.

Although chili peppers were unheard of in Europe until Columbus's fifteenth-century discovery, they had already played a major part in Asian cuisine for some 2,000 years. With the increase in shipping during the sixteenth and seventeenth centuries, Indian and Chinese flavorings spread around the globe. Chilies soon became a favorite way to add piquancy to cooking, especially because they were much cheaper than pepper.

Chilies have never fallen out of favor, and today around 25 percent of the world's population enjoy them in their daily diet. There is a huge variety to choose from, including Thai, Scotch bonnet, habanero, and jalapeño. They are grown widely in many parts of the world as an important commercial crop, but India is the biggest cultivator, exporter, and consumer of this hot pod.

As well as their fiery flavors, chilies also have many nutritional and health-boosting benefits. The pod's heat-emitting chemical compound, capsaicin, has antibacterial, anticarcinogenic, and pain-relieving properties, and may also lower bad cholesterol. Fresh red and green chilies are a rich source of vitamins A, B, and C, as well as minerals such as iron, potassium, magnesium, and copper.

Chilies can be bought fresh, dried, or powdered. Fresh varieties come in vibrant colors of red, green, orange, and yellow, and you should look for firm, plump ones with healthy stems. Avoid buying chilies that are soft, discolored, missing their caps, or have spots or signs of mold. Store them in the refrigerator or a cool, dark place for up to two weeks, then wash before use. The most flavorful dried chili peppers are the sun-dried variety. Look for ones with smooth, unblemished skins with a slight bendiness to them. Use within a year.

SPICES IN COOKING

Spices comprise all the dried parts, except the leaves, of a tropical plant or tree, such as the seeds, bark, roots, and berries. Popular spices, which are used to enrich the flavors of culinary ingredients, include mustard, pepper, paprika, cloves, cinnamon, ginger, and nutmeg, to name just a few of them.

As well as their appealing aromatic properties, many spices are renowned for their healing attributes. For example, turmeric is thought to be an excellent anti-inflammatory. Cloves aid digestion and have anti-bacterial properties, while ginger helps stave off nausea.

Spices may be dry-fried in a hot wok or saucepan or ground first with a mortar and pestle, then mixed into a paste with a little water. Once spices are ground, their flavor does begin to deteriorate, so it's preferable if you can grind your own—using a mortar and pestle or coffee grinder—immediately before cooking for optimum flavor. If this is not possible, store your ground spices in a cool place and use within six months of purchase.

CHILI PREPARATION

To decide whether a chili is mild or hot, first examine its shape. Milder chilies tend to have broader shoulders and blunter tips, whereas hotter ones have narrower shoulders and more pointy tips. Chilies of the same variety can vary in heat intensity. To test before adding to your recipe, try halving the chili and hold it just under your nose. If you feel a buzz, then you know it's a hot one.

Be careful when preparing chilies. The fiery heat comes from the chemical compound capsaicin,

which is located in the white pithy inner core or rib of the chili. Contrary to popular belief, the seeds don't actually contain any heat, but, because they lie close to the pith, they may acquire a layer of the hot compound. Capsaicin can aggravate skin and eyes so it is important to wash hands thoroughly after handling. If you want to reduce the intensity of a chili's heat, then remove the pith and seeds. If it is still too hot to handle, then you can try stirring in some yogurt, sour cream, or ghee to help take it down a notch.

We hope you enjoy your chili and spice journey. On the pages that follow, you will find an impressive range of recipes with the characteristic tastes and flavors of many different types of chilies and spices, from the spices star anise and nutmeg to jalapeño and Scotch bonnet chilies.

APPETIZERS & SNACKS

Prepare to tantalize your taste buds with this enticing selection of piquant hors d'oeuvres and nibbles. The mouthwatering flavors include hot Tabbouleh-Stuffed Jalapeños, Grilled Harissa Shrimp Skewers, Little Curried Crab Cakes, Ultimate Nachos with Beef, protein-packed Spice-Roasted Edamame & Cranberries, and the delectably addictive Five-Spice Cashews.

TABBOULEH-STUFFED JALAPEÑOS

MAKES: 48	PREP TIME: 22 mins	COOK TIME: 10–12 mins

JALAPEÑO PEPPERS ARE SMALL IN SIZE BUT CAN PACK A PUNCH WITH FLAVOR AND NUTRITION. PART OF THE NIGHTSHADE FAMILY, THESE LITTLE PEPPERS DERIVE THEIR HEAT FROM A NATURAL COMPOUND CALLED CAPSAICIN, KNOWN TO OFFER POWERFUL HEALTH BENEFITS.

INGREDIENTS

⅓ cup quinoa

2 cups chopped fresh parsley

2½ cups chopped fresh mint

2½ cups chopped fresh cilantro

1 preserved lemon, chopped

1 tbsp chopped walnuts

1 cup pomegranate arils

24 jalapeños, halved and deseeded

2 avocados, peeled, pitted, and sliced

juice of 1 lemon

salt and pepper (optional)

1. To make the tabbouleh, cook the quinoa according to the package directions. Drain and refresh under cold water, then drain again. Put into a large bowl.

2. Add the parsley, mint, cilantro, preserved lemon, walnuts, and pomegranate arils and mix thoroughly. Season with salt and pepper, if using.

3. Spoon the tabbouleh into the jalapeños. Top each one with a few slices of avocado, then squeeze the lemon juice over them to serve.

VARIATION
FOR A DIFFERENT TOPPING, TRY A TABLESPOON OF HUMMUS SPRINKLED WITH TOASTED SUNFLOWER SEEDS AND SMOKED PAPRIKA.

1 2
3

VEGETABLE SAMOSAS

| **MAKES:** 14 | **PREP TIME:** 40–45 mins, plus resting | **COOK TIME:** 1 hr |

IT TAKES A LITTLE PRACTICE TO MASTER SHAPING THESE INDIAN PASTRIES. MAKE SURE YOU SIMMER THE FILLING MIXTURE UNTIL IT IS DRY BEFORE USING.

INGREDIENTS

2 cups all-purpose flour

½ tsp salt

1½ tbsp clarified butter or butter

1½ tsp lemon juice

⅓–½ cup cold water

1 tbsp butter, for greasing

vegetable or peanut oil, for deep-frying

FILLING

¼ cup clarified butter, vegetable oil, or peanut oil

1 onion, minced

2 garlic cloves, crushed

1 potato, finely diced

2 carrots, finely chopped

2 tsp mild, medium, or hot curry powder, to taste

1½ tsp ground coriander

1 tsp ground turmeric

1 fresh green chili, deseeded and finely chopped

1 tsp salt

½ tsp black mustard seeds

1¼ cups cold water

⅔ cup frozen peas

⅓ cup finely chopped cauliflower florets

1. To make the filling, put the butter or oil into a large skillet over medium–high heat. Add the onion and garlic and sauté for 5–8 minutes, until soft. Stir in the potato and carrots and cook for 5 minutes. Stir in the spices, chili, salt, and mustard seeds. Pour in the water and bring to a boil. Reduce the heat to low and simmer, uncovered, for about 15 minutes. Add the peas and cauliflower and simmer until the vegetables are tender and the liquid has evaporated. Remove from the heat and set aside.

2. Meanwhile, sift the flour and salt into a bowl. Make a well in the center, add the butter and lemon juice, and work them into the flour. Gradually add the water until the mixture comes together to form a soft dough, and knead for about 10 minutes, until smooth. Shape into a ball, cover with a damp dish towel, and let rest for 15 minutes.

3. Divide the dough into seven pieces. On a lightly greased work surface, roll each piece of dough into an 8-inch circle, then cut in half to make two semicircles. Keep the remaining pieces of dough covered.

4. Working with one semicircle at a time, wet the edges with water. Place 2 teaspoons of filling on the dough, just off-center. Fold one side into the center, covering the filling. Fold the other side in the opposite direction, overlapping the first fold to form a cone shape. Wet the open edge with water and press to seal.

5. Heat the oil for deep-frying in a saucepan or deep fryer until it reaches 350–375°F. Working in batches, deep-fry the samosas for 2–3 minutes, flipping them over once, until golden brown. Remove with a slotted spoon and drain well on paper towels. Serve warm or at room temperature.

SPICY ONION FRITTERS

SERVES: 4	PREP TIME: 10–15 mins	COOK TIME: 25–30 mins

THESE SERIOUSLY TASTY, SPICED ONION FRITTERS ARE EXTREMELY DIFFICULT TO RESIST! THEY ARE A POPULAR STREET SNACK ALL OVER INDIA AND ARE BEST ENJOYED WITH VARIOUS CHUTNEYS FOR DIPPING.

INGREDIENTS

1½ cups chickpea flour

1 tsp salt, or to taste

small pinch of baking soda

2½ tbsp rice flour

1 tsp fennel seeds

1 tsp cumin seeds

2 fresh green chilies, finely chopped (deseeded if you like)

2 large onions, sliced into semicircles and separated

⅓ cup finely chopped fresh cilantro (both leaves and stems)

1 cup cold water

vegetable oil or peanut oil, for deep-frying

1. Sift the chickpea flour into a large bowl and add the salt, baking soda, rice flour, fennel seeds, and cumin seeds. Mix together well, then add the chilies, onions, and cilantro. Gradually pour in the water and mix until a thick batter is formed and the onions are thoroughly coated with it.

2. Heat enough oil for deep-frying in a large saucepan or deep fryer to 350–375°F, or until a cube of bread browns in 30 seconds. Add as many small amounts (each about 1½ teaspoons) of the batter as will fit in a single layer, without overcrowding the pan. Reduce the heat slightly and cook the fritters for 8–10 minutes, until golden brown and crisp.

3. Use a slotted spoon to remove the fritters from the oil and drain well on paper towels. Continue frying until all the batter mixture has been used. Serve hot.

GRILLED HARISSA SHRIMP SKEWERS

| SERVES: 4 | PREP TIME: 20 mins, plus 30 mins marinating | COOK TIME: 4–6 mins |

THESE HOT, TUNISIAN-INSPIRED SHRIMP SKEWERS ARE GREAT AS PART OF A SHARING PLATTER OR AS AN APPETIZER. YOU WILL NEED FOUR WOODEN SKEWERS.

INGREDIENTS

8 oz raw jumbo shrimp, peeled and deveined, thawed if frozen

2 tsp rose harissa

1 tsp fine sea salt

2 garlic cloves, finely chopped

¼ cup fresh cilantro, freshly chopped

2 tbsp olive oil

pinch of sea salt flakes

1 lemon, cut into wedges, to serve

1. Mix together the shrimp, rose harissa, fine sea salt, garlic, and half the cilantro in a large bowl. Cover and marinate in the refrigerator for 30 minutes.

2. Soak four wooden skewers in water for 20 minutes, then drain well. Thread the shrimp onto the skewers and brush them lightly with the oil.

3. Heat a ridged grill pan or heavy skillet over high heat until smoking hot. Lay the skewers on the pan, reduce the heat slightly, and cook for 4–6 minutes, or until pink and cooked through, turning halfway.

4. Serve the skewers immediately, sprinkled with the remaining cilantro and sea salt flakes, with lemon wedges for squeezing over them.

LITTLE CURRIED
CRAB CAKES WITH
AVOCADO SALAD

MAKES: 8	PREP TIME: 20 mins	COOK TIME: 8 mins

ONCE YOU'VE DONE THE PREPARATION, THESE LITTLE CRAB CAKES ARE EASY TO PUT TOGETHER, AND THEY ARE PERFECTLY COMPLEMENTED BY THE TANGY, CHILI-INFUSED AVOCADO SALAD.

INGREDIENTS

10½ oz white crabmeat

1 cup drained canned corn

1 cup whole wheat panko
bread crumbs

1 extra-large egg, beaten

1½ tbsp light mayonnaise

1½ tbsp fat-free plain
Greek yogurt

2 tbsp chopped fresh chives

2 tsp dijon mustard

1 tsp curry powder

¼ tsp pepper

10 sprays cooking spray,
for oiling

SALAD

1 large ripe avocado

1 tomato, finely chopped

juice of ½ lime

small bunch of fresh cilantro,
leaves only

½ fresh red jalapeño,
deseeded and finely chopped

3 scallions, chopped

1. Mix together the crabmeat, corn, bread crumbs, egg, mayonnaise, yogurt, chives, mustard, curry powder, and pepper in a bowl.

2. Using your hands, shape the mixture into eight patties. Spray a nonstick skillet with cooking spray to coat, then heat to just below medium-hot and add the patties to the pan. Cook the patties for 4 minutes, without turning or moving them.

3. Meanwhile, make the salad. Pit, peel, and slice the avocado, then lightly crush it in a bowl. Add the tomato, lime juice, cilantro leaves, chili, and scallions, and stir to combine.

4. Spray the tops of the patties with more cooking spray, then use a metal spatula to turn each one over carefully. Cook for an additional 3 minutes, or until the crab cakes are golden and piping hot. Serve immediately, topped with the avocado salad.

1 2

3

CHILI PEPPERS & THE SCOVILLE SCALE

Chili peppers are a small variety of Capsicum, a genus of tropical pepper plants distinctive for their heat. Ranging from green and yellow to orange, red, and black, there are more than 200 varieties.

The oil that creates the heat in chilies is called *capsaicin*. The amount of this oil in individual chilies can vary dramatically, even within the same chili type. The piquancy or hotness of chili peppers is measured using the Scoville scale, with units measured as SHU. This scale measures how much capsaicin is present in a chili. So a sweet pepper scores 0, and a pimento scores 100–1,000, moving right up to the Carolina Reaper at 1,500,000–2,200,000 SHU.

The chilies shown within these pages include the following varieties:

Anaheim chilies are a milder variety of the New Mexico chili pepper. They have a lime-green pod in a long, slender shape and have a mild, sweet, peppery flavor. They measure 500–2,500 SHU.

New Mexico chilies are green chilies with a flavor that has been likened to an onion, with a subtle hint of sweetness and spiciness. They measure between 800–1,400 SHU on the heat scale.

Cherry bomb chilies are small, round, and the shape of a cherry. They have a pleasant sweetness and are 2,500–5,000 SHU.

Guajillo chilies, a dried form of the mirasol chili, have a refreshing sweet quality and a tart, fruity flavor and are 2,500–5,000 SHU.

Jalapeños can be used fresh or pickled and range from moderate to fiery heat, or 2,500–5,000 SHU. These chilies are dried and smoked to make chipotles that have a deep, sweet flavor.

Serrano chilies have a substantial heat kick, rating between 8,000 and 23,000 SHU. They are easy to use in salsas because they don't need steaming or peeling before use.

Tabasco chilies are small and hot and have a unique, smoky flavor that is the main contributor to the distinctive taste of Tabasco sauce. They measure 30,000–50,000 SHU.

Thai chilies, also sometimes known as bird's eye chilies, are small and powerful chilies that measure 50,000–100,000 SHU. They have a spicy, fruity taste and are often used in Southeast Asian cooking.

Habanero chilies have a subtle fruity flavor and measure 100,000–350,000 SHU, so avoid these unless you relish a meal that is blow-your-head-off hot.

Scotch bonnet chilies, also known as Caribbean red bell peppers, are lantern-shaped hot chilies that can be yellow, green, or red. They have a sweeter flavor than habanero and a powerful heat rating of 100,000–350,000 SHU.

Carolina reaper chilies are currently the world's hottest pepper, measuring 1,500,000–2,200,000 SHU. The chili has a scorpion's tail and a sweet, fruity flavor before the heat hits.

2 3

5

CHIPOTLE TURKEY
CROQUETTES

MAKES: 16	PREP TIME: 35–40 mins	COOK TIME: 20–25 mins

THESE SUPERHOT CROQUETTES ARE BAKED INSTEAD OF BEING FRIED, AND THE LEAN TURKEY IS PACKED WITH HEALTHY MINERALS, SUCH AS IRON, ZINC, POTASSIUM, AND PHOSPHORUS.

INGREDIENTS

1–2 tbsp olive oil

4 scallions, quartered

1 small red bell pepper, deseeded and cut into chunks

1 carrot, shredded

2 tsp fresh thyme leaves

1 pound fresh ground turkey breast

🔥 1 fresh Carolina Reaper chili, minced

1 small dried chipotle chili, finely chopped

1 egg

1 tbsp cold water

⅓ cup freshly grated Parmesan cheese

½ cup golden flaxseed meal

sea salt and pepper (optional)

sprigs of fresh thyme, to garnish

AVOCADO DIP

1 large ripe avocado, halved and pitted

grated zest and juice of 1 lime

2 tbsp fat-free plain Greek yogurt

1. Preheat the oven to 400°F. Brush a baking sheet with a little of the oil and line with parchment paper. Finely chop the scallions and red bell pepper in a food processor. Add the carrot, thyme, and turkey, then sprinkle in the fresh and dried chilies and a little salt and pepper, if using. Process until evenly mixed.

2. Scoop out tablespoons of the mixture onto a cutting board to make 16 oval-shape mounds, then press them into neater shapes between your hands.

3. Lightly mix the egg, water, and a little salt and pepper together in a shallow dish. Mix the cheese and flaxseed in a separate shallow dish. Dip the croquettes, one at a time, into the egg, lift out with two forks, draining well, then roll in the cheese mixture. Place on the prepared baking sheet. Continue until all the croquettes are well coated.

4. Bake in the preheated oven for 20–25 minutes, until golden, turning halfway through cooking and brushing with the remaining oil, if needed. To check that they are cooked, cut one croquette in half—the juices will run clear with no traces of pink.

5. When the croquettes are almost ready to serve, make the dip. Scoop the avocado from the shell, mash with the lime juice and zest, and mix with the yogurt until smooth. Spoon into a small bowl set on a large plate, then arrange the hot croquettes around the dish, garnish with fresh thyme, and serve immediately.

STICKY TURKEY KABOBS

SERVES: 2	PREP TIME: 20 mins, plus 1 hr chilling	COOK TIME: 1 hr 30 mins

THE SOUTHWEST OF TURKEY IS WELL KNOWN FOR ITS SPICY KABOBS. HERE, GARLIC, GINGER, AND SOY COMBINE WITH THE PAPRIKA AND CUMIN IN THE SPICY RUB TO GIVE THESE KABOBS A GENTLE KICK.

INGREDIENTS

10 oz turkey breast, cubed

2 cups cooked long-grain rice, to serve

salad greens, to garnish

SPICE RUB

1 tbsp packed dark brown sugar

¼ tsp paprika

¼ tsp ground cumin

¼ tsp salt

¼ tsp pepper

STICKY SAUCE

1 tbsp vegetable oil

1 onion, finely chopped

2 garlic cloves, finely chopped

1-inch piece ginger, grated

3 tbsp ketchup

3 tbsp white wine or apple cider vinegar

3 tbsp soy sauce

2 tbsp packed light brown sugar

1 cup water

1. Put the turkey into a bowl and add the spice rub ingredients, mixing well to coat. Chill in the refrigerator for at least 1 hour.

2. Meanwhile, make the sauce. Heat the oil in a saucepan over medium heat. Add the onion, garlic, and ginger and cook for 5 minutes. Add the ketchup, wine vinegar, soy sauce, sugar, and water and bring to a boil. Reduce the heat and simmer for 1 hour, stirring regularly, until the mixture is thick and sticky.

3. If using wooden skewers, soak them in water for 30 minutes to prevent them from burning. Preheat the grill or broiler to hot. Thread the turkey pieces onto skewers and lay them on a sheet of aluminum foil. Set aside some of the sticky sauce for serving, then brush a little of the sticky sauce on the kabobs. Cook the kabobs on the grill or under the broiler for 10–15 minutes, turning and brushing with more of the sticky sauce until cooked. Serve with the rice and the reserved sticky sauce, garnished with salad greens.

STICKY BOURBON CHICKEN WINGS

| SERVES: 4 | PREP TIME: 20 mins | COOK TIME: 20–30 mins |

PAPRIKA IS THE KEY SPICE PLAYER HERE, BUT IT HAS THE HELP OF ITS FRIENDS GROUND CUMIN, WORCESTERSHIRE SAUCE, CHIPOTLE PASTE, AND, LAST BUT NOT LEAST, BOURBON. REPLACE THE BOURBON WITH APPLE JUICE IF YOU PREFER.

INGREDIENTS

2¼ lbs chicken wings, tips removed

1 tbsp vegetable oil, for brushing

RUB

1 tbsp paprika

½ tsp ground cumin

1 tsp dried thyme

1 tsp dried oregano

1 tsp salt

1 tsp pepper

BOURBON GLAZE

2 tbsp bourbon

2 tbsp apple cider vinegar

1 tbsp Worcestershire sauce

2 tbsp molasses

2 tbsp ketchup

2 tbsp chipotle paste

1 tbsp mustard

½ tsp salt

½ tsp pepper

1. To make the rub, combine all the ingredients in a large bowl.

2. Cut each chicken wing in half. Add the wing pieces to the bowl containing the rub and turn until coated thoroughly.

3. To make the bourbon glaze, put a medium saucepan over medium heat. Add the bourbon and flambé. When the flames have disappeared, add the remaining glaze ingredients and simmer over medium heat until the sauce has reduced by half.

4. Prepare the grill for direct cooking and preheat to medium–hot.

5. Thread half of the chicken wing pieces onto two metal skewers, creating a raft shape. Repeat with the remaining wings. Brush the wings with the bourbon glaze.

6. Lightly brush the barbecue rack with the oil and cook the wings for 10 minutes on each side, brushing with more glaze as they cook.

7. Cook until the chicken is tender and the juices run clear when the tip of a sharp knife is inserted into the thickest part of the meat. The meat should come away easily from the bone. Remove from the skewers and serve.

MASALA
SHRIMP CAKES

| **MAKES:** 20 | **PREP TIME:** 20 mins, plus 6–8 hrs chilling | **COOK TIME:** 12–15 mins |

PERFECT AS HORS D'OEUVRES, THESE SHRIMP CAKES ARE PACKED WITH THE PUNCHY, FRESH FLAVORS OF GARLIC, GINGER, COCONUT, CHILI, CILANTRO, AND MINT. SQUEEZE A LITTLE LIME JUICE OVER THEM AND SERVE WITH A CHILLED DRINK.

INGREDIENTS

1¾ lbs raw jumbo shrimp, peeled and deveined

2 fresh red chilies, deseeded and minced

⅓ cup finely chopped fresh cilantro

⅓ cup finely chopped fresh mint

1 tsp coconut cream or coconut milk

4 scallions, finely sliced

2 garlic cloves, finely chopped

2 tsp finely grated fresh ginger

½ cup fresh white bread crumbs

2 tsp ground cumin

1 tsp chili powder

1 medium egg, lightly beaten

¼ cup vegetable oil or peanut oil

lime wedges, to serve

1. Coarsely chop the shrimp and put them into a food processor with the remaining ingredients, apart from the oil. Blend to a coarse paste. Transfer the mixture to a bowl, cover, and chill in the refrigerator for at least 6–8 hours, or overnight.

2. Preheat the oven to 400°F. Line a baking sheet with parchment paper.

3. Shape the fish mixture into 20 small patties, about 1½ inches in diameter. Place on the prepared baking sheet and lightly brush with the oil. Bake in the preheated oven for 12–15 minutes, or until slightly puffed up and light golden.

4. Serve warm or at room temperature with lime wedges for squeezing over.

ULTIMATE NACHOS
WITH BEEF

SERVES: 2	PREP TIME: 10 mins	COOK TIME: 30 mins

WHEN YOU'RE EXPECTING CHILI-LOVERS FOR DINNER, THIS IS A REALLY QUICK AND EASY DISH TO SERVE. THE SAUCE IS SPICY HOT, SO IT WILL KEEP YOUR TONGUE FIRED UP, AND ANY LEFTOVERS MAKE A DELICIOUS TACO FILLING.

INGREDIENTS

2 tbsp olive oil

1 onion, chopped

8 oz fresh ground beef

1 tbsp dried oregano

1 tbsp paprika

1 tbsp ground cumin

1½ cups tomato puree or tomato sauce

1 cup water

2 tbsp butter

¼ cup all-purpose flour

2 cups milk, warmed

1 cup shredded cheddar cheese,

1 cup shredded Monterey Jack cheese

1 tbsp mustard

⅔ cup grated Parmesan cheese

1 (8 oz) package tortilla chips

1 ripe avocado

¾ cup drained pickled jalapeños

1 small red onion, finely chopped

salt and pepper (optional)

1. In a medium saucepan, heat the oil over medium–high heat and add the onion. Cook for 5 minutes, or until translucent and slightly golden. Add the meat and cook for an additional 5 minutes, breaking up the meat with a wooden spoon until it starts to brown.

2. Add the oregano, paprika, cumin, tomato puree, and water, and cook over low heat for 20 minutes, or until reduced by half. Season with salt and pepper, if using, and set aside, keeping warm.

3. Meanwhile, melt the butter in a medium saucepan, add the flour, and mix well with a wooden spoon. Slowly add the warm milk, trying to keep any lumps from forming, until the sauce thickens and starts to boil. Turn off the heat and add the cheddar cheese, Monterey Jack cheese, mustard, and half the Parmesan cheese. Stir until smooth, season with salt and pepper, if using, and set aside.

4. Ladle half the cooked beef over a large serving platter. Place the tortilla chips on top, followed by the rest of the meat, then top with the cheese sauce.

5. Cut the avocado in half and remove the pit, then peel and chop into small pieces. Spread the avocado pieces over the nachos along with the jalapeños, chopped red onion, and the remaining Parmesan cheese. Serve immediately.

2 3

3

SPICY OVEN-BAKED COATED EGGS

| SERVES: 4 | PREP TIME: 25 mins | COOK TIME: 30 mins |

THESE SAUSAGE-COATED EGGS ARE PACKED WITH FLAVOR BUT ARE LOWER IN FAT AND SIMPLER TO PREPARE THAN THE ORIGINAL PICNIC FARE KNOWN AS SCOTCH EGGS, INVENTED BY LONDON DEPARTMENT STORE FORTNUM AND MASON.

INGREDIENTS

4 extra-large eggs

1 tbsp oil, for greasing

10½ oz sausage, casing removed

1 tbsp mild curry paste

1 tsp onion seeds

2 tbsp fresh flat-leaf parsley leaves, coarsely chopped

1 cup fresh white bread crumbs

2 tbsp milk

tomato relish, to serve

1. Put the eggs into a saucepan and cover with cold water. Bring to a boil, then remove from the heat. Cover the pan and let stand for 6 minutes. Drain and cool under cold running water, then carefully peel off the shells.

2. Preheat the oven to 375°F. Lightly grease a baking sheet or line with nonstick parchment paper. Put the sausage meat, curry paste, onion seeds, and parsley into a bowl. Mix well. Add the bread crumbs and milk and mix again. Divide into four equal portions.

3. Lay a piece of plastic wrap on the work surface. Place one-quarter of the sausage mixture on top and flatten with clean hands to a diameter of about 5 inches. Place an egg in the center and use the plastic wrap to lift and mold the mixture around it. Smooth over the edges to seal. Place on the baking sheet. Repeat with the remaining sausage mixture and eggs.

4. Bake in the preheated oven for 25 minutes, until lightly browned, and serve with tomato relish.

SPICE-ROASTED EDAMAME & CRANBERRIES

SERVES: 4	PREP TIME: 15 mins	COOK TIME: 15 mins

FROZEN EDAMAME OR YOUNG SOYBEANS MAKE A HEALTHY, PROTEIN-PACKED SNACK, AND THEIR HIGH LEVELS OF FIBER KEEP YOU FEELING FULLER LONGER.

INGREDIENTS

2 cups frozen edamame (soybeans)

2-inch piece fresh ginger, peeled and finely grated

1 tsp szechuan peppercorns, coarsely crushed

1 tbsp soy sauce

1 tbsp olive oil

3 small star anise

⅓ cup dried cranberries

1. Preheat the oven to 350°F. Put the beans into a roasting pan, then sprinkle with the ginger and peppercorns, drizzle with soy sauce and oil, and mix together.

2. Tuck the star anise in among the beans, then roast, uncovered, in the preheated oven for 15 minutes.

3. Stir in the cranberries and let cool. Spoon into a small jar and eat within 12 hours.

TIP
EDAMAME BEANS ARE EXTREMELY VERSATILE AND PACK A MUCH GREATER NUTRITIONAL PUNCH THAN FROZEN PEAS.

FIVE-SPICE CASHEWS

SERVES: 8	PREP TIME: 5 mins	COOK TIME: 10–12 mins

PEPPERCORNS, STAR ANISE, FENNEL, CLOVES, AND CINNAMON COMBINE HERE WITH THE NATURAL SWEETNESS OF CASHEWS. THIS NUTTY CONCOCTION MAKES A DELIGHTFUL SNACK OR APPETIZER.

INGREDIENTS

1 tbsp peanut oil, for greasing

½ tsp szechuan peppercorns

2 star anise

½ tsp fennel seeds

6 whole cloves

½ tsp ground cinnamon

2 tbsp water

¼ cup firmly packed light brown sugar

1 tsp salt

2 cups unsalted, toasted cashews

1. Preheat the oven to 400°F. Lightly grease a baking pan and a large piece of aluminum foil.

2. In a spice grinder, grind together the peppercorns, star anise pods, fennel seeds, and cloves until finely ground. Add the cinnamon and mix well.

3. Put the water and sugar into a medium saucepan and heat over medium heat, stirring constantly, for 2 minutes, or until the sugar has dissolved. Add the spice mixture and salt and stir to mix well. Add the cashews and stir to coat completely. Cook, stirring, for an additional minute.

4. Transfer the cashews to the prepared pan and spread out in an even layer. Roast in the preheated oven for 6–8 minutes, until most of the liquid has evaporated. Then transfer the cashews to the prepared foil and separate them so that they don't stick together. Let cool completely before serving.

5. Store in an airtight container at room temperature for up to two weeks.

LIGHT MEALS & FAST FARE

Looking for a light lunch or supper or a speedy,
satisfying solution when you're short on time? Then this
warming range of flavorful recipes should hit the spot.
From hearty soups and fresh salads to spicy omelets
and tacos, each dish promises to satisfy your appetite.
How about Vegetable Noodle Broth, Chili Squid with
Watercress, or a Spicy Fish Stick Sandwich?

CHICKEN SOUP
WITH CHILI & COUSCOUS

SERVES: 4	PREP TIME: 20 mins	COOK TIME: 1¾ hrs

THE BROTH FOR THIS TRADITIONAL MIDDLE EASTERN SOUP IS MADE WITH A WHOLE CHICKEN, WHICH IS THEN TORN INTO STRIPS BEFORE BEING ADDED BACK TO THE SOUP. LEBANESE SEVEN SPICE IS A MIXTURE OFTEN USED IN DISHES WITH GROUND BEEF OR LAMB, AS WELL AS POULTRY.

INGREDIENTS
1 tbsp olive oil

2 onions, finely chopped

1 red chili, deseeded and finely chopped

1 tsp ground cumin

1 tsp paprika

1 tsp granulated sugar

2 tsp dried mint

1 tbsp tomato paste

½ cup couscous

3 tbsp finely chopped fresh cilantro, to garnish

1 lemon, cut into wedges, to serve

BROTH
1 (3 lb) ready-to-cook chicken

1 onion, quartered

1 lemon, quartered

⅓ cup fresh parsley stems

1 tsp coriander seeds

1 cinnamon stick

pinch of sea salt

pinch of pepper

1. To make the broth, put the chicken, onion, lemon, parsley stems, coriander seeds, and cinnamon stick into a deep saucepan and pour in just enough water to cover. Bring to a boil, then reduce the heat to medium–low, cover, and simmer for 1 hour, or until the chicken is almost falling off the bone. To check if it is cooked, pierce the thickest part of the thigh with the tip of a sharp knife. Any juices should be piping hot and clear with no traces of red or pink.

2. Transfer the chicken to a large plate and let cool slightly. Meanwhile, simmer the broth until it has reduced to about 5 cups. Season with the salt and pepper, then strain into a bowl. Remove the skin from the chicken and tear the meat into strips.

3. Heat the oil in a heavy saucepan over medium heat. Add the onions and chili and sauté for 2–3 minutes, stirring often. Stir in the cumin, paprika, sugar, mint, and tomato paste, then pour in the broth. Bring to a boil, then gradually stir in the couscous. Reduce the heat to medium–low and simmer for 15 minutes. Stir in the cooked chicken strips and simmer for 5 minutes.

4. Serve the soup in shallow bowls, garnished with the cilantro and lemon wedges for squeezing over the top.

SPICY LENTIL & CARROT SOUP

SERVES: 4	PREP TIME: 15 mins	COOK TIME: 45–50 mins

RED LENTILS ARE NOT ONLY A GOOD SOURCE OF PROTEIN BUT ALSO THE PERFECT FOOD FOR ABSORBING STRONG, SPICY FLAVORS.

INGREDIENTS

⅔ cup red lentils

5 cups vegetable broth or stock

6 carrots, sliced

2 onions, chopped

1 cup canned diced tomatoes

2 garlic cloves, chopped

2 tbsp oil

1 tsp ground cumin

1 tsp ground coriander

1 fresh green chili, deseeded and chopped

½ tsp ground turmeric

1 tbsp lemon juice

1¼ cups milk

2 tbsp chopped fresh cilantro

salt and pepper (optional)

TO SERVE

4 tsp plain yogurt

naan or other flatbread

spicy popadams

1. Put the lentils into a large saucepan, together with 3¾ cups of the broth or stock, the carrots, onions, tomatoes, and garlic. Bring the mixture to a boil, then reduce the heat, cover, and simmer for 30 minutes, or until the vegetables and lentils are tender.

2. Meanwhile, heat the oil in a separate saucepan. Add the cumin, ground coriander, chili, and turmeric and cook over low heat for 1 minute. Remove from the heat and stir in the lemon juice. Season with salt, if using.

3. Remove the soup from the heat and let cool slightly. Transfer to a food processor or blender, in batches if necessary, and process until smooth. Return the soup to the rinsed-out pan, add the spice mixture and the remaining broth or stock, and simmer over low heat for 10 minutes.

4. Add the milk, taste, and adjust the seasoning, adding salt and pepper if using. Stir in the chopped cilantro and reheat gently; do not boil. Ladle into warm bowls and serve immediately with yogurt, naan, and spicy popadams.

SPICY CHICKPEA RED PEPPER SOUP

| SERVES: 4 | PREP TIME: 15 mins | COOK TIME: 25 mins |

CHICKPEAS HAVE BEEN SHOWN TO HELP REGULATE BLOOD SUGAR AND IMPROVE SATIETY AFTER A MEAL, MAKING THEM A HEARTY INGREDIENT IN THIS TASTY SOUP.

INGREDIENTS

2½ tbsp olive oil

6 scallions, chopped

1 large fresh red jalapeño, deseeded and finely sliced

4 garlic cloves, finely chopped

2 tsp ground cumin

1 tsp chili powder

3 fresh ripe tomatoes, peeled and coarsely chopped

2¼ cups roasted red peppers in water, drained and thinly sliced

1 tbsp red pepper pesto

4 cups reduced-sodium vegetable broth or stock

2½ cups drained and rinsed, canned chickpeas

1 tsp sugar

2 tsp red wine vinegar

3½ cups baby spinach

pepper (optional)

4 thick slices bread, to serve

1. Heat the oil in a large saucepan over medium heat. Add the scallions and cook for 2–3 minutes, stirring occasionally, until soft.

2. Add the chili, garlic, cumin, and chili powder and cook for 1 minute, stirring.

3. Stir in the tomatoes, roasted red peppers, pesto, and broth or stock and bring to a simmer. Cook for 10 minutes, then add the chickpeas, sugar, vinegar, and pepper, if using, and cook for an additional 5 minutes.

4. Stir in the spinach and cook for 1 minute, until the spinach wilts. Serve with bread.

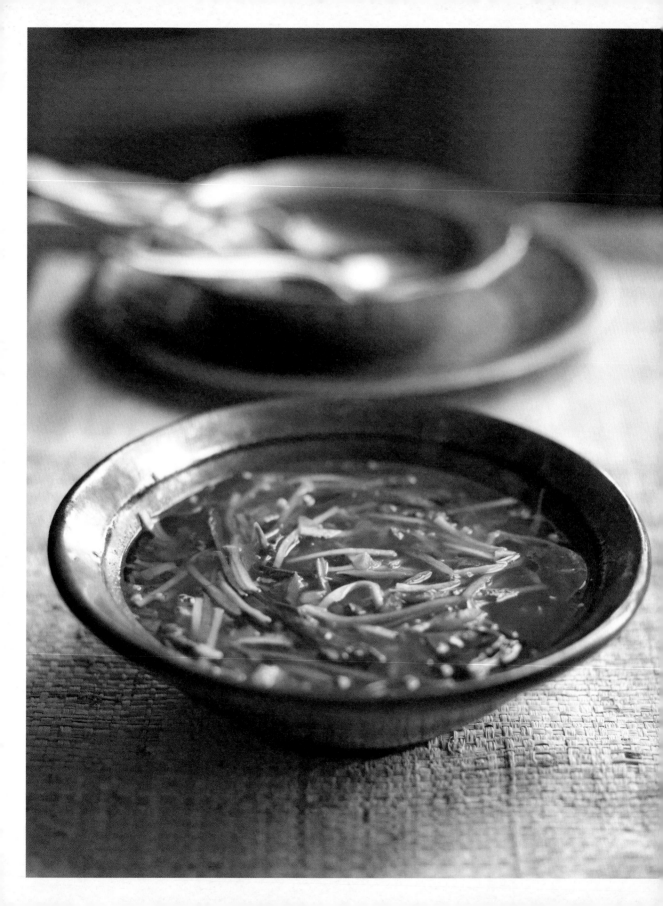

VEGETABLE NOODLE BROTH

SERVES: 4	PREP TIME: 25–30 mins	COOK TIME: 25–30 minutes

THIS HEARTY VEGETARIAN VERSION OF A POPULAR NOODLE-BASED BROTH IS A GOOD EXAMPLE OF THE INFLUENCE OF TIBETAN CUISINE IN THE BENGAL REGION.

INGREDIENTS

16 oz dried thick egg noodles

2 tbsp vegetable oil or peanut oil

1 onion, finely chopped

1 tsp ground cumin

½ tsp ground turmeric

2 garlic cloves, crushed

2 tsp grated fresh ginger

1 tsp salt

2 fresh green chilies, finely chopped

1 cup thinly sliced snow peas (sliced lengthwise)

2 large carrots, cut into matchsticks

1 red bell pepper, deseeded and thinly sliced

2 tomatoes, finely chopped

2 tbsp dark soy sauce

4 cups vegetable broth

1 tsp pepper

7 cups baby spinach

⅓ cup finely chopped fresh cilantro

1 tsp toasted sesame oil

1. Cook the noodles according to the package directions. Drain, rinse with cold water, and set aside.

2. Meanwhile, heat the vegetable oil in a large saucepan over medium heat. Add the onion, and sauté for 8–10 minutes, or until lightly browned.

3. Add the cumin, turmeric, garlic, ginger, salt, and chilies to the pan and cook for 1–2 minutes. Add the snow peas, carrots, and red bell pepper and sauté for an additional 1–2 minutes.

4. Add the tomatoes, soy sauce, broth, and pepper. Bring to a boil, then reduce the heat and simmer for 10–12 minutes, until the vegetables are tender.

5. Add the reserved noodles and the spinach and bring back to a boil. Stir until the spinach wilts, then remove from the heat and stir in the chopped cilantro and sesame oil. Ladle into bowls and serve immediately.

HOT & SOUR
ZUCCHINI

SERVES: 4	PREP TIME: 15 mins, plus 20 mins draining	COOK TIME: 5 mins

THIS SIMPLE DISH HAS A MEDIUM-HOT PUNCH OF TASTY APACHE CHILI. THE ZUCCHINI CAN BE PREPARED AS A VEGETABLE SIDE DISH OR AS A DELICIOUS LIGHT SNACK WITH CRUSTY BREAD OR SESAME NOODLES.

INGREDIENTS

2 large zucchini, thinly sliced

1 tsp salt

2 tbsp peanut oil

1 tsp szechuan peppercorns, crushed

1 red Apache chili, deseeded and sliced into thin strips

1 large garlic clove, thinly sliced

½ tsp finely chopped fresh ginger

1 tbsp rice vinegar

1 tbsp light soy sauce

2 tsp sugar

1 scallion, green part included, thinly sliced

a few drops of sesame oil, to garnish

1 tsp sesame seeds, to garnish

1. Put the zucchini slices into a large colander and toss with the salt. Cover with a plate and put a weight on top to press out the water in the zucchini. Let drain for 20 minutes. Rinse off the salt and spread out the slices on paper towels to dry.

2. Preheat a wok over high heat and add the peanut oil. Add the peppercorns, chili, garlic, and ginger. Cook for about 20 seconds, until the garlic is just beginning to brown.

3. Add the zucchini slices and toss in the oil. Add the rice vinegar, soy sauce, and sugar and stir-fry for 2 minutes. Add the scallion and cook for 30 seconds. Garnish with the sesame oil and sesame seeds and serve immediately.

PREPARING CHILIES

Chilies, especially the hotter ones, need to be handled carefully because the capsaicin, which creates the heat, is an irritant. Soak or toast chilies to enhance their flavor and make them easier to use.

Managing chili heat

The capsaicin in a chili provides the heat and, as a rule, the smaller and thinner a chili is, the hotter it will taste. A chili's capsaicin is produced in a gland running down the middle of the fruit and this is the hottest part, although the seeds themselves are not that hot. If you deseed the chili and remove the membrane, you can reduce the heat.

Capsaicin is an oil and will stick to your skin, so be careful when chopping chilies, especially if you are removing the gland or the seeds. If your skin is sensitive, wear plastic gloves and never touch your eyes or mouth after handling chilies without first thoroughly washing your hands with soap and water. You can also protect your hands by first rubbing them with vegetable oil, which acts as an effective barrier.

Panfrying chilies can release a potent vapor that may irritate your eyes, so set the exhaust fan to high before starting, or open a window.

If the heat of a chili is too much in your mouth, don't drink a glass of water, which spreads the heat around. Reach, instead, for milk or yogurt, because dairy helps to dilute the heat more effectively.

Toasting chilies

Toasting both fresh and dried chilies endows them with a depth of flavor that will create a much richer final dish. To toast chilies, cook them in a dry skillet over medium heat until you can smell their aroma.

Press large chilies, such as guajillos and pasillas, with a metal spatula against the hot surface until they puff up and soften. Smaller chilies, such as pequin, should be stirred constantly so they don't burn. You want blackened and blistered skins, but don't over-toast them or they will taste bitter. Immediately remove them from the pan and set aside.

Another technique is to put the chilies on a baking sheet in an oven, preheated to 425°F, for 5 minutes, or until the chilies slightly puff up and soften.

Soaking chilies

Many recipes specify soaking chilies so they are soft enough to blend. This can mean softening fresh chilies or rehydrating dried ones. You can do this by putting the chilies into a heatproof bowl and covering them with boiling water. Let stand for 5 minutes, until the chilies are softened and flexible. Smaller chilies, such as Thai and chipotle, will need to be weighed down with a small saucepan lid or heatproof plate to keep them submerged. Strain the chilies well, then pat dry and remove the stems. If you want to reduce the heat of the chilies, seed and remove the membrane before soaking them.

Never throw away the liquid you soak your chilies in. It is full of flavor and is great for giving a kick to soups, stews, and gravies. Let it cool, then transfer to an airtight container and store in the refrigerator. Or for the especially organized, freeze in an ice-cube tray, then transfer the individual cubes to a freezer-proof bag.

CHILI SQUID
WITH WATERCRESS

| SERVES: 4 | PREP TIME: 4 mins, plus chilling | COOK TIME: 4 mins |

HERE IS A SALAD THAT IS BOTH COOL AND HOT, CONSISTING OF FRESH SALAD GREENS, STIR-FRIED SQUID, AND EXTRA-HOT THAI CHILIES.

INGREDIENTS

12 squid tubes and tentacles (about 1½ lbs), cleaned and prepared

2–3 tbsp olive oil

2 Thai red chilies, deseeded and thinly sliced

2 scallions, finely chopped

lemon wedges, for squeezing, plus extra to serve

3 handfuls of watercress

2 handfuls of baby spinach or arugula

freshly ground black pepper (optional)

DRESSING

½ cup olive oil

juice of a lime

2 shallots, thinly sliced

1 medium tomato, peeled, deseeded, and finely chopped

1 garlic clove, crushed

freshly ground black pepper

1. To make the dressing, mix the oil, lime juice, shallots, tomato, and garlic together in a bowl, season with pepper, then cover and refrigerate until required.

2. Cut the squid tubes into 2-inch pieces, then lightly score diamond patterns with the tip of a sharp knife. Heat the oil in a wok or large skillet over high heat, add the squid pieces and tentacles, and stir-fry for 1 minute. Add the chilies and scallions and stir-fry for an additional minute. Season with pepper, if using, and add a good squeeze of lemon juice.

3. Mix the watercress and spinach together, then toss with enough of the dressing to coat lightly. Serve immediately with the squid, together with lemon wedges to squeeze over the dish.

TIP
IF YOU CAN, CHOOSE FRESH, OPEN BUNCHES OF WATERCRESS INSTEAD OF THOSE THAT ARE PACKAGED IN SEALED BAGS.

1 2
2

EGGPLANT PAPRIKA SALAD

SERVES: 4	PREP TIME: 15 mins	COOK TIME: 20 mins

THIS WARM SALAD IS A SATISFYING WAY TO EAT EGGPLANTS, BRINGING YOU SMOKY FLAVORS, A VARIETY OF TEXTURES, AND WARMING SPICES, ALL TOGETHER ON THE SAME PLATE.

INGREDIENTS

2 eggplants

2 tbsp olive oil

2 red bell peppers, deseeded and cut into 6 pieces each

2½ cups drained and rinsed, canned chickpeas

1 red onion, finely chopped

4 whole wheat pitas, to serve

DRESSING

3 tbsp olive oil

juice of ½ lemon

1 tsp ground coriander

1 tsp ground cumin

2 tsp smoked paprika

1 tsp sugar

small bunch of fresh cilantro, leaves removed and reserved and stems chopped

salt and pepper (optional)

1. Preheat the broiler to high. Cut the eggplants lengthwise into ½-inch-thick slices, brush with oil on both sides, and arrange on a broiler rack. Add the red bell pepper pieces. Cook under the preheated broiler until the eggplants are charred in patches on the top side; turn over and cook until the eggplants are soft and the red bell pepper pieces are lightly cooked and slightly blackened in places. Remove from the heat but do not turn off the broiler. Cut the eggplant slices into large bite-size pieces and put into a shallow serving dish with the red bell pepper pieces, chickpeas, and red onion.

2. To make the dressing, combine the oil, lemon juice, ground coriander, cumin, paprika, and sugar with salt and pepper, if using, in a small bowl. Add the cilantro stems to the dressing and stir to combine. Spoon the dressing evenly over the salad and stir—it's best to do this while the vegetables are still warm.

3. Meanwhile, lightly toast the pitas under the broiler.

4. Sprinkle the salad with the reserved cilantro leaves and serve with the pitas.

SHAKSHUKA EGGS
WITH SPICY
TOMATO SAUCE

SERVES: 4	PREP TIME: 10 mins	COOK TIME: 35 mins

ORIGINATING IN NORTH AFRICA, SHAKSHUKA IS A WARMING AND SAVORY BREAKFAST DISH. IT IS DELICIOUS SERVED WITH A HUNK OF CRUSTY BREAD TO HELP MOP UP THE JUICES.

INGREDIENTS
1 tsp cumin seeds
1 tsp coriander seeds
2 tsp olive oil
1 onion, finely chopped
4 cups canned plum tomatoes
¼ cup chili pesto
pinch of saffron
¼ tsp cayenne pepper
½ tsp salt
1 tsp pepper
3 tbsp chopped fresh cilantro
4 extra-large eggs

1. Crush the cumin seeds and coriander seeds. Put a nonstick skillet over medium heat and add the seeds to the pan. Stir for 1 minute, or until their aromas are released.

2. Reduce the heat to medium–low, add the oil, and heat. Add the onion and cook, stirring occasionally, for 5 minutes, or until the onion is soft and just turning slightly golden.

3. Add the tomatoes, breaking up any large ones, pesto, saffron, cayenne pepper, and salt and pepper. Stir well, bring to a simmer, and cook for 15 minutes, adding a little hot water toward the end if the pan looks too dry (but you don't want the sauce to be too runny). Stir in half of the fresh cilantro.

4. Make four wells in the sauce and break an egg into each one. Cover the pan and cook over low heat for 10 minutes, or until the egg whites are set but the yolk is still runny. Sprinkle the remaining fresh cilantro over the top and serve immediately.

AVOCADO, BACON & CHILI FRITTATA

SERVES: 4	PREP TIME: 15 mins	COOK TIME: 14 mins

INSPIRED BY THE MEXICAN FLAVORS OF CHILIES AND AVOCADO, THIS PROTEIN-PACKED FRITTATA IS WONDERFUL LINGERED OVER ON A LAZY MORNING. YOU CAN MAKE IT AHEAD AND STORE IT IN THE REFRIGERATOR FOR TWO DAYS.

INGREDIENTS

8 bacon strips, coarsely chopped

6 eggs, beaten

3 tbsp heavy cream

2 large avocados, peeled, pitted, and sliced

1 fresh red Mexican poblano chili (or, for a hotter option, 1 serrano), deseeded and thinly sliced

½ lime

sea salt and pepper (optional)

1. Cook the bacon in a skillet over high heat, stirring, for 4–5 minutes, or until crisp and golden. Using a slotted spoon, transfer to a plate lined with paper towels. Remove the skillet from the heat.

2. Pour the eggs into a bowl, add the cream, and season with salt and pepper, if using, then beat. Return the pan to the heat. When it is hot, pour in the egg mixture and cook for 1–2 minutes, without stirring. Sprinkle the bacon and avocado on top and cook for an additional 2–3 minutes, or until the frittata is almost set and the underside is golden brown.

3. Put the frittata under the broiler and cook for 3–4 minutes, or until the top is golden brown and the egg is set. Sprinkle with the chili and squeeze the juice of the lime half over the top. Cut into wedges and serve.

TIP
THE SOFT TEXTURE OF THE FRITTATA WORKS BEST WITH REALLY CRISPY BACON, SO COOK THE BACON OVER MEDIUM HEAT UNTIL IT NO LONGER HAS ANY PINK, WHITE, OR TRANSLUCENT SPOTS.

EGG WHITE OMELET WITH SPICY FILLING

| SERVES: 1 | PREP TIME: 10 mins | COOK TIME: 10 mins |

RICH IN PROTEIN AND FIBER, AN EGG WHITE OMELET IS AN EASY AND SATISFYING LUNCH, ESPECIALLY WHEN STUFFED WITH A TASTY, SPICY FILLING.

INGREDIENTS

4 egg whites

¼ tsp salt

1 tbsp water

2 tsp oil from a jar of sun-dried tomatoes

2 scallions, finely chopped

⅓ cup rinsed, canned mixed beans, such as kidney beans, pinto beans, and black-eyed peas

¼ cup frozen corn, thawed

¼ cup hot tomato salsa

3 sun-dried tomatoes in oil, drained and chopped

½ tsp smoked paprika

½ tsp pepper

2 tbsp chopped fresh cilantro

cooking oil spray, for greasing

1. Put the egg whites into a bowl with the salt and water and beat together.

2. Put the oil into a small skillet over medium heat. Add the scallion and sauté for 1 minute, until soft.

3. Add the beans and corn to the pan with the salsa, tomatoes, paprika, and pepper. Cook for a few minutes, then stir in half of the cilantro. Set the mixture aside and keep warm.

4. Spray a separate small skillet with the cooking oil and heat over high heat until hot. Pour in the egg white mixture and cook, making sure that the egg cooks evenly. When the underside is golden and the top is cooked but still moist, spoon the bean filling over the top, then sprinkle over the remaining chopped cilantro.

5. Tip the pan gently to one side, fold the omelet in half, and slide out onto a warm serving plate. Serve immediately.

1   3
4

STUFFED CHILI BHAJIS

MAKES: 8	PREP TIME: 20 mins, plus soaking	COOK TIME: 10 mins

THIS SNACK OF CHILIES STUFFED WITH A SPICED POTATO MIXTURE IS A CENTRAL INDIAN SPECIALTY AND A TRADITIONAL STREET FOOD. SERVE IT WITH YOUR FAVORITE CHUTNEY OR PLAIN YOGURT.

INGREDIENTS

8 large, mild fresh green chilies, halved and deseeded

vegetable oil or peanut oil, for deep-frying

BATTER

2¾ cups chickpea (besan) flour

¾ cup rice flour

½ tsp baking powder

1 tsp ground cumin

2 tsp salt

1 tsp chili powder

about 3 cups cold water

STUFFING

2 tbsp vegetable oil or peanut oil

1 tsp fennel seeds

2 tsp black mustard seeds

1 tsp cumin seeds

1 potato, peeled, boiled, and mashed

3 tbsp finely chopped fresh cilantro

1 tsp salt

½ tsp tamarind paste

1 tbsp roasted peanuts, coarsely chopped

1. Soak the chilies in boiling water for 5 minutes. Drain on paper towels and set aside.

2. Mix together the batter ingredients with enough of the water to make a thin batter with the consistency of heavy cream. Set aside.

3. To make the stuffing, heat the oil in a saucepan. Add the fennel seeds, mustard seeds, and cumin seeds. When the seeds start to pop, add the potato, cilantro, and salt and mix well. Add the tamarind paste and sprinkle the roasted peanuts over the potato mixture. Remove from the heat and mash until evenly combined. Let cool until the potato mixture is no longer too hot to touch.

4. Using your fingers, stuff the green chilies with the potato mixture.

5. Heat enough oil for deep-frying in a large saucepan or deep fryer to 350–375°F, or until a cube of bread browns in 30 seconds. Working in batches, dip the stuffed green chilies in the batter and deep-fry for 2–3 minutes, or until crisp and golden. Remove with a slotted spoon and drain on paper towels. Serve warm.

SPICY FISH STICK SANDWICH

SERVES: 2	PREP TIME: 10 mins	COOK TIME: 10 mins

FOR AN INSTANT SPICY SNACK, PREPARE SOME STANDARD FISH STICKS, THEN FLAVOR THEM WITH A RUSSIAN DRESSING THAT HAS CREAMED HORSERADISH, SRIRACHA SAUCE, WORCESTERSHIRE SAUCE, AND PAPRIKA AS KEY INGREDIENTS.

INGREDIENTS

oil for deep-frying

20 fish sticks

4 large slices white bread

3½ cups arugula

RUSSIAN DRESSING

2 tbsp mayonnaise

1 tbsp creamed horseradish

1 tbsp ketchup

1 tbsp sour cream

1 tbsp sriracha sauce

1 tsp Worcestershire sauce

½ tsp smoked paprika

1. Heat enough oil for deep-frying in a large saucepan or deep fryer to 350–375°F, or until a cube of bread browns in 30 seconds.

2. Meanwhile, mix together all of the Russian dressing ingredients in a small bowl and set aside.

3. Deep-fry the fish sticks in batches of 10 for 5 minutes or until golden, then remove with a slotted spoon, drain on paper towels, and let rest in a warm place while you cook the remaining fish sticks. Alternatively, prepare the fish sticks according to package directions.

4. Spread some of the dressing on two of the bread slices. Divide the fish sticks between two slices of bread and drizzle with the rest of the dressing. Top with the arugula and the remaining bread slices and serve immediately.

1 2
3

TURKEY
PAPRIKA TACOS

| **SERVES:** 4 | **PREP TIME:** 15 mins, plus 30 mins marinating | **COOK TIME:** 8 mins |

TURKEY MAKES A REFRESHING CHANGE FROM CHICKEN IN ALMOST ANY DISH, AND ITS SOMEWHAT RICHER FLAVOR LENDS ITSELF WELL TO MEXICAN-STYLE MEALS SUCH AS THIS ONE.

INGREDIENTS
10½ oz skinless, boneless turkey breasts, cut into strips

2 garlic cloves, crushed

2 tsp smoked paprika

juice of ½ lime

1 red onion, chopped

1 tomato, chopped

½ cup cooked black beans

2 cups shredded crisp lettuce

4 whole wheat tortillas

⅓ cup shredded cheddar cheese

2 tsp hot sauce

½ cup sour cream

1. Put the turkey strips into a shallow bowl. Stir in the garlic with the paprika and lime juice. Cover and let marinate for 30 minutes.

2. Meanwhile, combine the onion, tomato, beans, and lettuce in a bowl.

3. Preheat the broiler to medium–hot. Line a baking pan with foil. Put the turkey strips onto the prepared pan and cook under the preheated broiler for about 6 minutes, turning once, until golden and cooked through. Set aside.

4. Heat the tortillas under the broiler until slightly golden and crisp. Divide the turkey and the bean mixture evenly among the tortillas, arranging them on only one half of the tortilla. Sprinkle with the cheese and drizzle with hot sauce and sour cream. Fold the tacos to serve.

HOT SAUCES & RUBS

Add a spicy, hot intensity to any dish with this diverse choice of flaming sauces and rubs. The international range of sauces, from Mexican salsa to Caribbean jerk sauce, can be used as marinades or dips or can be served alongside seafood and meat dishes. From Hot-as-Hell Horseradish to Sweltering Satay and Ketchup with a Kick, there's sure to be a sauce to set you on fire.

SPICY SALSA

| **MAKES:** about 2 cups | **PREP TIME:** 10 mins | **COOK TIME:** 20 mins |

THIS SALSA PROVIDES A SPICY ACCOMPANIMENT TO ANY MEXICAN MEAL AND IS ESPECIALLY GOOD ON BURRITOS. THE FRESH TASTE OF THE CILANTRO, LIME JUICE, AND ONION SUCCESSFULLY OFFSET THE HEAT OF THE JALAPEÑOS.

INGREDIENTS

vegetable oil spray

8 plum tomatoes, halved

2–4 jalapeños, to taste, halved, cored, and deseeded

4 garlic cloves

1 large onion, cut into wedges

½ cup fresh cilantro

¼ cup lime juice

1 tsp salt

1. Preheat the oven to 450°F and spray a baking sheet with oil.

2. Place the tomatoes, jalapeños, garlic, and onion on the prepared baking sheet and lightly spray with oil. Sprinkle with a little salt and roast in the preheated oven for 15–20 minutes, until the vegetables soften and begin to brown.

3. Put the vegetables into a food processor and pulse to a chunky paste. Add the cilantro, lime juice, and 1 teaspoon of salt and pulse until the cilantro is chopped and all of the ingredients are well combined.

4. To store, cover and refrigerate for up to one week.

RED-HOT
GARLIC & CHILI OIL

MAKES: about 1 cup	**PREP TIME:** 5 mins	**COOK TIME:** 2 hrs

CHILI OIL CAN BE USED TO SPICE UP DISHES, WHETHER DRIZZLING OVER PIZZAS OR PASTA OR ADDING A SPLASH TO MEXICAN-STYLE BEEF CHILI. THE LONGER YOU LET THE OIL SETTLE, THE HOTTER IT WILL BE.

INGREDIENTS

5 garlic cloves, halved lengthwise

2 tbsp jalapeño, deseeded and chopped

1 tsp dried oregano

1 cup canola oil

1. Preheat the oven to 300°F. Combine the garlic, chili, and oregano with the oil in an ovenproof measuring cup. Put into an ovenproof dish in the center of the oven and heat for 1½–2 hours. The temperature of the oil should reach 250°F.

2. Remove from the oven, let cool, then strain through cheesecloth into a clean jar. Store in an airtight container in the refrigerator for up to one month. Alternatively, you can leave the garlic and chili pieces in the oil and strain before using.

KETCHUP
WITH A KICK

| **MAKES:** about 2½ cups | **PREP TIME:** 15 mins | **COOK TIME:** 2 hrs 15 mins |

THIS IS A GREAT RECIPE FOR THE TIME WHEN TOMATOES ARE AT THEIR CHEAPEST AND MOST PLENTIFUL. MAKE UP LARGE BATCHES OF THIS KETCHUP AND ENJOY THE TASTE OF SUMMER ALL YEAR ROUND.

INGREDIENTS

20 ripe, juicy tomatoes (about 5 pounds), coarsely chopped

2 red jalapeños, coarsely chopped

1 sweet white onion, coarsely chopped

1 tsp salt

1 tsp fennel seeds

1 tsp black mustard seeds

1 cup apple cider vinegar or white wine vinegar

½ cup firmly packed light brown sugar

1 cinnamon stick

½ tsp ground nutmeg

½ tsp sweet paprika

1–3 tsp cayenne pepper

1–2 tbsp tomato paste (optional)

pepper (optional)

1. Put the tomatoes, chilies, onion, and salt into a large saucepan over high heat. Stir until the tomatoes begin to break down, then reduce the heat to low, cover, and simmer for 30 minutes, or until the tomatoes are pulpy.

2. Meanwhile, put the fennel seeds and mustard seeds on a square of cheesecloth, bring the sides together, tie to make a bag, then set aside.

3. Pass the tomato mixture through a strainer into a large saucepan, rubbing back and forth with a wooden spoon and scraping the bottom of the strainer to produce as much paste as possible.

4. Add the spice, vinegar, sugar, cinnamon stick, nutmeg, paprika, and cayenne pepper. Season with pepper, if using, then stir until the sugar dissolves. Bring to a boil, then reduce the heat and simmer, uncovered, for 1½ hours, skimming the surface as necessary, until the sauce is reduced and thickened. Transfer to a bowl and let cool.

5. Depending on how flavorful the tomatoes are, you might want to add some tomato paste. Remove the spice bag and cinnamon stick.

6. Let the ketchup cool completely. Use immediately, or store in an airtight container in the refrigerator for up to one month. It can also be frozen for up to three months.

HOT & FIERCE
GOCHUJANG SAUCE

MAKES: about ⅔ cup	**PREP TIME:** 5 mins	**COOK TIME:** none

KOREAN COOKS USED TO MAKE ENOUGH GOCHUJANG, A FERMENTED CHILI AND SOYBEAN PASTE, IN THE SPRING TO LAST A FAMILY ALL YEAR. USE THIS SAUCE AS A MARINADE OR DIPPING SAUCE, OR FOR BASTING MEAT AND POULTRY.

INGREDIENTS

⅓ cup gochujang paste

2 tsp chili paste

2 tbsp sugar

2 tbsp hot water

2 tsp light soy sauce

1 tsp rice vinegar

1 tsp toasted sesame oil

1. Combine the gochujang paste, chili paste, and sugar in a heatproof bowl, then add the water, stirring to blend and dissolve the sugar and paste.

2. Stir in the soy sauce, vinegar, and sesame oil. Let the sauce cool completely.

3. The sauce can be used immediately, or stored in an airtight container in the refrigerator for up to two weeks.

TIP
THIS RECIPE COMBINES AUTHENTIC FLAVOR WITH THE SPEED OF USING FERMENTED BEAN AND CHILI PASTE FROM AN ASIAN GROCERY STORE.

INTENSE TEXAS
CHILI SAUCE

MAKES: about 3 cups	**PREP TIME:** 10 mins	**COOK TIME:** 25 mins

TEXAS CHILI—OR "BIG RED" AS THE LOCALS KNOW IT—IS NOT MADE WITH BEANS, JUST MEAT, SO IT NEEDS A TASTY SAUCE LIKE THIS THAT HAS PLENTY OF HEAT AND FLAVOR.

INGREDIENTS

2 tbsp sunflower oil or canola oil

1 red onion, chopped

2 large garlic cloves, chopped

1 green serrano chili, halved lengthwise

1 tbsp packed dark brown sugar

2 tsp ground cumin

2 tsp dried Mexican oregano or dried thyme

2 dried morita chipotle chilies, toasted, soaked, deseeded, and chopped

1 dried guajillo chili, toasted, soaked, deseeded, and chopped

1 dried New Mexico red chili, toasted, soaked, deseeded, and chopped

1 (14½ oz) can diced tomatoes

½ cup beef broth or stock

½ cup strong black coffee

salt and pepper (optional)

1. Heat the oil in a saucepan over medium–high heat. Add the onion and sauté for 3–5 minutes, or until soft. Add the garlic, serrano chili, sugar, cumin, and oregano and cook for an additional minute.

2. Transfer the onion mixture to a food processor or blender. Add the chipotle chilies, guajillo chili, New Mexico chili, tomatoes, broth or stock, and coffee, and season with salt and pepper, if using. Process until pureed, scraping down the side of the processor, if necessary.

3. Transfer the puree to the pan and bring to a boil. Reduce the heat to low, cover, and simmer for 15 minutes, stirring occasionally.

4. The sauce can be used immediately, or cooled and stored in an airtight container in the refrigerator for up to three days. This sauce can be frozen for up to three months.

TEXAS-STYLE CHILI

| **SERVES:** 4 | **PREP TIME:** 10 mins | **COOK TIME:** 3 hrs |

TEXANS DON'T TOLERATE BEANS OR ANY OTHER ADDITIONS IN THEIR BIG BOWLS OF CHILI. WHAT YOU SEE IS WHAT YOU GET—JUST CHUNKS OF BEEF AND HOT CHILI SAUCE. IT'S PLAIN AND SIMPLE AND UTTERLY DELICIOUS.

INGREDIENTS

2 tbsp rendered bacon fat, sunflower oil, or canola oil, plus extra, if needed

1½ lbs beef chuck steak, cut into 1-inch cubes

1 large onion, finely chopped

1 large garlic clove, finely chopped

1 tbsp crushed red pepper flakes

3 cups Intense Texas Chili Sauce (see page 77)

1 tbsp masa harina

1 tbsp red wine vinegar

salt and pepper (optional)

cooked rice and sour cream, to serve

1. Heat the fat in a large, heavy saucepan over medium heat. Season the beef with salt and pepper, if using. Working in batches, add the beef to the pan and cook, stirring occasionally, until brown on all sides, adding extra fat, if needed. Remove the beef from the pan and reserve all but one tablespoon of fat and juices.

2. Add the onion to the pan and cook for 3–5 minutes, or until soft. Add the garlic and red pepper flakes and cook for an additional minute. Return the beef and the reserved juices to the pan and stir in the Texas Chili Sauce. Cover and bring to a boil, then reduce the heat to low and simmer for 2¼–2½ hours, until the beef is tender.

3. Put the masa harina into a small bowl and stir in the vinegar. Stir the mixture into the chili and simmer for 10 minutes, or until the chili thickens. Season with salt and pepper. Serve in bowls over rice, topped with sour cream.

CHIMICHURRI
SWELTERING SAUCE

MAKES: about ¾ cup	**PREP TIME:** 5 mins, plus 3 hrs chilling	**COOK TIME:** none

NO LATIN AMERICAN BARBECUE IS COMPLETE WITHOUT A BOWL OF ZINGY, FRESH CHIMICHURRI, A BLEND OF HERBS AND CHILIES. THIS HOT-AND-SPICY VERSION HAS A THAI CHILI TO CRANK UP THE HEAT. SERVE WITH GRILLED AND ROASTED MEATS OR A SELECTION OF VEGETABLE STICKS.

INGREDIENTS

¾ cup fresh cilantro leaves

⅔ cup fresh flat-leaf parsley leaves

4 garlic cloves, coarsely chopped

1–2 green Thai chilies, finely chopped

1 tsp crushed red pepper flakes

1 tsp dried Mexican oregano or 1 tsp dried thyme (optional)

½ cup sunflower oil or canola oil

¼ cup red wine vinegar or white wine vinegar

salt and pepper, to taste

1. Put the cilantro, parsley, garlic, chilies, red pepper flakes, oregano, if using, and salt and pepper into a food processor and finely chop, scraping down the sides if necessary. Do not blend to a paste.

2. With the motor running, slowly drizzle in the oil. Add the vinegar and adjust the seasoning if necessary.

3. The sauce can be used immediately, but is best if you store it in an airtight container in the refrigerator for at least 3 hours to let the flavors blend. The sauce will keep for up to three days in the refrigerator if covered with an extra layer of oil, although its bright green color will dull. Pour off the oil before serving.

TIP
IF YOU DON'T WANT TO USE A FOOD PROCESSOR, FINELY CHOP THE CILANTRO, PARSLEY, AND GARLIC, THEN MIX TOGETHER IN A NONMETALLIC BOWL.

JAMAICAN JERK
SAUCE

| **MAKES:** about 1¼ cups | **PREP TIME:** 10 mins, plus 30 mins marinating | **COOK TIME:** none |

THIS HOT, HOT, HOT CARIBBEAN FAVORITE CAN BE USED AS A MARINADE OR AS A BASTING SAUCE WHILE BARBECUING. CHICKEN IS ITS TRADITIONAL PARTNER, BUT IT ALSO ADDS A SUNNY CARIBBEAN TASTE TO MOST MEAT AND SEAFOOD DISHES.

INGREDIENTS

¼ cup freshly squeezed lemon juice

¼ cup dark soy sauce

¼ cup sunflower oil

¼ cup red wine vinegar or white wine vinegar

4 red Scotch bonnet chilies or habanero chilies, deseeded and finely chopped

4 scallions, finely chopped

1 shallot, finely chopped

1-inch piece fresh ginger, grated

2 tbsp packed light brown sugar

2 tsp dried thyme

1 tsp ground allspice

½ tsp ground cinnamon

¼ tsp ground cloves

salt and pepper

1. Mix together the lemon juice, soy sauce, oil, and vinegar in a large bowl.

2. Stir in the remaining ingredients and season with salt and pepper, stirring until the sugar dissolves. Set aside for at least 30 minutes for the flavors to blend.

3. The sauce can be used immediately, or stored in an airtight container in the refrigerator for up to one month.

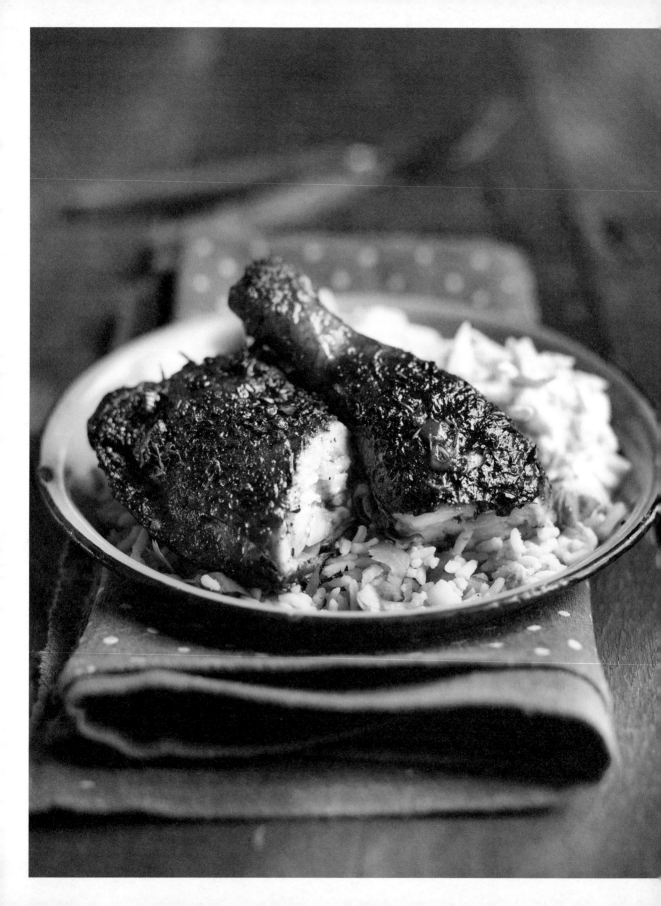

JERK CHICKEN

| SERVES: 4 | PREP TIME: 10 mins, plus 4 hrs marinating | COOK TIME: 40 mins |

AUTHENTIC JAMAICAN JERK CHICKEN HAS A UNIQUE FLAVOR FROM BEING SLOWLY COOKED OVER PIMENTO OR ALLSPICE WOOD. WHILE THE FLAVOR HERE ISN'T EXACTLY THE SAME, IT DOES GIVES YOU THE JAMAICAN JERK HEAT.

INGREDIENTS

4 chicken legs

1¼ cups Jamaican Jerk Sauce (see page 81)

sunflower oil, for brushing

coleslaw, pineapple, and rice salad, to serve (optional)

1. Use a fork to pierce the chicken legs all over. Put the chicken into a bowl in a single layer. Pour the Jamaican Jerk Sauce over the poultry and rub in. Cover the bowl with plastic wrap and marinate in the refrigerator for at least 4 hours, or for up to 36 hours.

2. Remove the chicken from the refrigerator 30 minutes in advance of cooking. Light a grill and heat until the coals turn gray. Alternatively, preheat the broiler to high and oil the broiler rack.

3. Place the chicken pieces on the rack, bone side up. Brush with some of the sauce remaining in the bowl and cook for 20 minutes.

4. Turn the chicken over and cook for an additional 20 minutes, brushing with the remaining sauce, or until it is cooked all the way through and the juices run clear when the thickest part of the chicken is pierced with a sharp knife.

5. Transfer the chicken to a warm plate and let rest for 5 minutes. Use a cleaver or large knife to cut each leg into two pieces, then serve with coleslaw, pineapple, and rice salad, if using.

LOUISIANA
HOT PEPPER SAUCE

MAKES: about ½ cup	**PREP TIME:** 5 mins	**COOK TIME:** 15 mins

THIS SAUCE IS TRADITIONALLY MADE WITH FRESH, SMALL TABASCO CHILIES, BUT THEY CAN BE DIFFICULT TO FIND, SO DRIED CAYENNE OR THAI CHILIES ARE USED IN THIS RECIPE TO GIVE IT ZING.

INGREDIENTS

2 oz dried red cayenne peppers or dried red Thai chilies, stems removed, coarsely chopped, and soaked for 30 minutes

½ cup white wine vinegar

½ tsp salt

1. Turn the exhaust fan to high or open a window to let air circulate. Drain the soaked chilies. Put the chilies, vinegar, and salt into a small saucepan. Cover the pan and bring to a boil, then reduce the heat to low and simmer for 10–12 minutes, or until soft.

2. Tip the contents of the pan into a small food processor or blender and puree, scraping down the side of the processor if necessary. Strain the blended mixture to remove the seeds. Transfer the sauce to a bowl and let cool completely.

3. Let the sauce mature for at least 2 weeks in an airtight container in the refrigerator before using. The sauce will then keep in the refrigerator for an additional month.

PIQUANT PICO DE GALLO SAUCE

MAKES: about ¾ cup	**PREP TIME:** 10 mins, plus 30 mins resting	**COOK TIME:** none

HOT AND FRESH FLAVORS MINGLE IN THIS SIMPLE MEXICAN SALSA-LIKE SAUCE, WHICH ADDS A BURST OF CHILI HEAT TO EVERYTHING FROM A BOWL OF TORTILLA CHIPS TO GRILLED MEAT TO TACOS.

INGREDIENTS

⅔ cup tomato puree or tomato sauce

2 tbsp freshly squeezed lime or orange juice, or to taste

2 large pickled garlic cloves or fresh garlic cloves, minced

½ sweet white onion, finely chopped

2 tbsp pickled jalapeños, drained and finely chopped

½ tsp ancho chili powder

salt and pepper (optional)

small handful of cilantro leaves, finely chopped, to garnish

1. Combine the tomato puree or sauce and lime juice in a bowl and season with salt and pepper, if using. Add all the remaining ingredients, except the cilantro leaves.

2. The sauce can be served immediately, but it will benefit from resting at room temperature for 30 minutes for the flavors to blend. Stir well before serving and adjust the lime juice and salt and pepper, if using. Sprinkle with cilantro just before serving.

3. If there is any leftover sauce, pour a layer of olive oil over it, cover, and store in the refrigerator for up to three days. Stir in the oil just before serving and garnish with chopped fresh cilantro.

TIP
STILL NOT HOT ENOUGH? THEN USE RED OR GREEN THAI CHILIES INSTEAD OF THE JALAPEÑOS.

INGREDIENTS
FOR HOT SAUCES

With a little judicious selection, common pantry ingredients can produce an astonishing variety of flavors in your sauces. Use the ingredients below and experiment to suit your taste.

Chilies are the essential ingredient in most hot sauce recipes, and they come in a wide range of varieties and heats.

Harissa paste is a strong and aromatic dark red paste (see opposite, top left) made from chilies, spices, and herbs, used for adding heat and flavor to North African food. The base ingredients are chilies, garlic, oil, ground cumin, coriander, and caraway seeds.

Herbs and spices provide a depth of flavor, whether they are fresh or dried. Jamaican Jerk Sauce, for example, wouldn't taste authentic without dried allspice, and Chimichurri Sweltering Sauce relies on a medley of fresh herbs.

Horseradish is a thick, white root that, when freshly grated, has an intense, sharp, hot flavor. Mixing grated horseradish with lemon juice helps prolong the sharpness. If buying grated horseradish, avoid horseradish sauce, which is mixed with cream, or grated horseradish in vinegar.

Mustard is one of the most popular and widely used spices and condiments and will add a hot punch to a meal. The level of heat is defined by the seed type and preparation. Choose bright yellow dry mustard for the hottest flavor.

Paprika is the finely ground powder of dried sweet red bell peppers—its heat ranges from mild and sweet to intensely hot. It needs to be fresh, otherwise the flavor is lost.

Oil is necessary for cooking chilies and other ingredients and for adding body to sauces. Keep a selection, such as sunflower, canola, peanut, and olive, to have a variety of flavor options on hand.

Salt is used to bring out individual flavors.

Sambal oelek paste is a red sauce (see opposite, bottom right) from Indonesia. It is made with chilies, salt, and citrus juice or vinegar; comes in varying degrees of hotness; and is sold in supermarkets and specialty food stores.

Szechuan peppercorns have an unmistakable flavor—the heat blends with a lingering tingling sensation on your tongue and cheeks (see opposite, bottom left).

Sugars, both white and brown, will provide a counterpoint to hot spiciness and act as a preservative. Always dissolve sugar before bringing a sauce to a boil to prevent crystals from forming.

Vinegar provides a sour background, as well as acts as a preservative. Traditional American sauces often contain distilled white vinegar, but apple cider vinegars, red wine vinegar, and white wine vinegar are also good.

Wasabi, also known as Japanese horseradish (see opposite, top right), comes from a root and packs a real punch. It is pungent and hot, and it is sold as a stem for grating, as well as already prepared as a paste or in powder form.

PERI-PERI AT YOUR PERIL SAUCE

MAKES: about ⅓ cup	**PREP TIME:** 10 mins	**COOK TIME:** 10 mins

THIS PERI-PERI SAUCE IS AS GOOD AS ANY YOU WOULD FIND AT WELL-KNOWN RESTAURANTS. YOU CAN PAIR IT WITH FRIED CHICKEN WINGS TO CREATE A DELICIOUS HOT-AND-SPICY MEAL.

INGREDIENTS

¼ cup sunflower oil

24 peri-peri chilies or Thai chilies, chopped

½ onion, finely chopped

4 large garlic cloves, chopped

1 tsp sweet paprika

¼ tsp ground allspice

⅓ cup freshly squeezed lemon juice, or to taste

2 tbsp water

finely grated zest of 1 lemon

salt and pepper (optional)

1. Turn the exhaust fan to high or open a window to let air circulate. Heat the oil in a saucepan over medium heat. Add the chilies and onion and cook for 3 minutes. Add the garlic, paprika, and allspice and stir for an additional minute.

2. Add ¼ cup of the lemon juice and the water and season with salt and pepper, if using. Bring to a boil, stirring. Reduce the heat to low, cover, and simmer for 5 minutes, or until the chilies are soft. Uncover and check once or twice to make sure the garlic doesn't burn.

3. If you would like a smooth, restaurant-style sauce, transfer the ingredients to a small food processor or blender and puree, or leave as a chunky sauce, if preferred. Stir in the remaining lemon juice. Adjust the seasoning and lemon juice, if desired. Stir in the lemon zest.

4. The sauce can be used immediately, or let it cool completely and store in an airtight container in the refrigerator for up to two weeks.

1   2
3

SPICY ROASTED TOMATO SAUCE

MAKES: about ¾ cup	**PREP TIME:** 10 mins	**COOK TIME:** 45 mins

THIS SAUCE, WITH ITS PAPRIKA AND SHERRY INGREDIENTS, HAS A SPANISH FLAVOR AND IS GREAT WHEN SERVED AS A DIP WITH TORTILLA CHIPS OR AS AN ACCOMPANIMENT TO A SPANISH OMELET OR FRENCH FRIES.

INGREDIENTS

6 vine-ripened tomatoes

1 red bell pepper, cut into quarters and deseeded

1 garlic clove, unpeeled

1 red onion, cut into quarters

¼ cup olive oil

1 small red jalapeño, minced

1 tsp hot paprika

1 tbsp sherry

salt and pepper, to taste

1. Preheat the oven to 350°F.

2. Lay out the vegetables on a large baking pan, brush with olive oil, then roast in the oven, turning once halfway through cooking, for about 45 minutes or until they are blistered and slightly charred.

3. Let cool. When cool enough to handle, peel the tomatoes and red bell pepper, and squeeze the garlic from its skin. Transfer the tomato, red bell pepper, garlic, and onion to a food processor and process to a fairly smooth consistency.

4. Spoon the mixture into a large serving bowl and stir in the chili, paprika, and sherry. Season with salt and pepper. The sauce can be used immediately or let it cool completely and store in an airtight container in the refrigerator for up to one week.

TIP
THE TABLESPOON OF SHERRY IN THIS RECIPE CAN ALSO BE REPLACED BY MADEIRA, WHICH IS A FORTIFIED WINE FROM PORTUGAL.

HABANERO
CHILI RUB

MAKES: about ⅔ cup	PREP TIME: 10 mins	COOK TIME: none

THE HABANERO CHILI IS ONE OF THE HOTTEST CHILIES IN THE WORLD, RATED 100,000–350,000 ON THE SCOVILLE SCALE. SO IF YOU'RE CHOOSING TO USE THIS RUB, BE PREPARED FOR YOUR TASTE BUDS TO TINGLE.

INGREDIENTS

2 tbsp paprika

1–2 tbsp dried crushed habanero chilies or chili powder

1 tbsp garlic powder

1 tbsp onion powder

1 tbsp ground cumin

1 tbsp salt

2 tsp pepper

2 tsp packed light brown sugar

1 tsp cayenne pepper

½ tsp freshly grated nutmeg

1. Mix all the ingredients together in a small bowl until thoroughly combined.

2. Rub the mixture thoroughly into meat, poultry, fish, or seafood 1–2 hours before cooking.

3. Put in a shallow dish, cover tightly, and chill in the refrigerator until required.

HOT-AS-HELL
HORSERADISH SAUCE

| MAKES: about ⅔ cup | PREP TIME: 10 mins | COOK TIME: none |

THIS EASY SAUCE GETS ITS PUNCHY HEAT FROM FRESHLY GRATED HORSERADISH. IT'S TRADITIONALLY ADDED TO SEAFOOD COCKTAILS, BUT YOU CAN ADD A SPOONFUL OR TWO TO HOMEMADE TOMATO SOUP FOR AN EXTRA KICK.

INGREDIENTS

½ cup ketchup, plus extra, if needed

1-inch piece horseradish, finely grated, or 1 tbsp grated horseradish

1 tbsp freshly squeezed lemon juice, or to taste, plus extra if needed

pepper (optional)

1. Put the ketchup and horseradish into a bowl and stir to combine.

2. Add the lemon juice and pepper, if using. Stir to combine, then add extra lemon juice if desired.

3. The sauce can be served immediately, or stored in an airtight container in the refrigerator for up to three weeks. After one or two days, the sauce will thicken, so you will need to beat in extra ketchup or lemon juice with a fork when ready to serve.

TIP
WHEN HORSERADISH IS GRATED IT CAN IRRITATE YOUR EYES—KEEP IT AT ARMS LENGTH AS YOU GRATE IT, AND ENSURE GOOD VENTILATION.

RAS EL HANOUT
CARIBBEAN RUB

MAKES: about ½ cup	**PREP TIME:** 10 mins	**COOK TIME:** none

COMBINE THIS HOT CARIBBEAN RUB WITH OIL TO USE AS A MARINADE OR BASTING SAUCE WHILE BARBECUING. TRADITIONALLY PAIRED WITH CHICKEN, IT ALSO ADDS A CARIBBEAN TASTE TO MEAT AND SEAFOOD DISHES.

INGREDIENTS
2 tsp ground cumin
2 tsp ground ginger
2 tsp ground turmeric
2 tsp ground cinnamon
2 tsp ground cardamom seeds
2 tsp ground coriander seeds
2 tsp ground ginger
2 tsp ground allspice
2 tsp saffron threads
1 tsp freshly grated nutmeg
1 tsp salt
1 tsp pepper
½ tsp ground cloves

1. Mix all the ingredients together in a small bowl until they are thoroughly combined.

2. Rub the mixture thoroughly into meat, poultry, fish, or seafood just before cooking.

3. Put in a shallow dish, cover tightly, and chill in the refrigerator until required.

RAS EL HANOUT, GARLIC & THYME ROAST LEG OF LAMB

SERVES: 6–8 | **PREP TIME:** 15 mins | **COOK TIME:** 3 hrs 30 mins, plus 30 mins resting

ROASTING THIS SPICED LEG OF LAMB SLOWLY WILL GIVE YOU MELTINGLY TENDER MEAT AND WILL FILL YOUR KITCHEN WITH WONDERFUL AROMAS.

INGREDIENTS

20 fresh lemon thyme sprigs

8 garlic cloves, peeled

4 tsp sea salt flakes

¼ cup Ras El Hanout Caribbean Rub (see page 93)

¼ cup olive oil

1 (4½–5½ lb) leg of lamb

2 heads of garlic, halved horizontally

2 onions, cut into quarters

1¼ cups water

salt and pepper, to serve

1 tbsp plain Greek yogurt, to serve

1. Preheat the oven to 300°F. Strip the leaves from half the lemon thyme and put them into a mortar and pestle. Add the garlic cloves and 3 teaspoons of the salt and crush. Add the ras el hanout and oil, and mix to form a coarse paste.

2. Put the lamb into a roasting pan. Using a sharp knife, make several small slits in the skin. Rub in the spice paste, working it into the slits well. Sprinkle with the remaining salt, put the halved heads of garlic and quartered onions alongside it, sprinkle with the remaining lemon thyme, and then pour the water around it.

3. Roast for 30 minutes, uncovered. Baste the lamb with the cooking liquid and cover the pan with aluminum foil. Roast for an additional 3 hours, basting every half an hour.

4. Transfer the lamb to a serving plate, add the onions and garlic, and let rest, covered in foil, for 30 minutes.

5. For the gravy, skim the excess oil off the liquid and season with a pinch of salt and pepper. Stir the yogurt into the gravy and serve alongside the roast lamb and onions.

RED-HOT GREEN SAUCE

| MAKES: about 1¾ cups | PREP TIME: 10 mins | COOK TIME: none |

THIS COMBINATION OF PICKLED JALAPEÑOS AND SMOKED HOT PAPRIKA PACKS A PUNCH, MAKING STORE-BOUGHT SALSA SEEM MILD AND UNEXCEPTIONAL! THE SAUCE IS ZESTY AND HOT, AND THE FRESH GREEN COLOR LOOKS APPETIZING IN A CONTRASTING BOWL.

INGREDIENTS

14 drained canned tomatillos (about 16 oz), stem ends removed, and coarsely chopped

4 scallions, chopped

2 large garlic cloves, coarsely chopped

2 tbsp drained pickled jalapeños, chopped

handful of cilantro leaves

freshly squeezed lime juice (optional)

1 tsp honey

½ tsp smoked hot paprika

salt and pepper (optional)

1 tbsp finely chopped fresh cilantro, to garnish

1. Put the tomatillos, scallions, garlic, chilies, and cilantro leaves into a food processor and process in short blasts to finely chop, but not puree.

2. Transfer the mixture to a bowl. Season with salt and pepper, if using, then add the lime juice, if using, and the honey. Stir in the paprika.

3. The sauce can be used immediately, or stored in an airtight container in the refrigerator for up to four days, although the color will start to dull after three days. Sprinkle with the chopped cilantro just before serving.

1 2

2

1 2
2

SWELTERING
SATAY SAUCE

SERVES: about ¾ cup	**PREP TIME:** 10 mins	**COOK TIME:** 5 mins

TRADITIONALLY MILD PEANUT SAUCE IS HEATED UP WITH THE ADDITION OF AN INDONESIAN CHILI PASTE CALLED SAMBAL OELEK. IT IS SOLD IN MOST ASIAN FOOD STORES BUT THE INTENSITY OF THE HEAT VARIES WITH THE BRAND.

INGREDIENTS

2 tbsp sunflower oil

2 shallots, finely chopped

1 large garlic clove, finely chopped

1-inch piece fresh ginger, finely chopped

1–3 tsp Indonesian chili paste (sambal oelek)

1 cup coconut milk

⅓ cup chunky peanut butter

1 tsp tamarind paste or freshly squeezed lime juice, or to taste

1 tsp dark soy sauce, or to taste

¼ cup water, if needed

4 red jalapeños, deseeded and thinly sliced

salt and pepper (optional)

1. Heat the oil in a wok over high heat until hot. Add the shallots, garlic, and ginger and stir-fry for 1–2 minutes, or until the shallots are soft and just beginning to brown. Stir in the chili paste and continue cooking for an additional 30 seconds.

2. Add the coconut milk and peanut butter, stirring until blended. Stir in the tamarind paste and soy sauce, season with pepper, if using, and continue stirring over medium heat for 2–3 minutes. If the mixture looks separated, stir in the water and beat well. Stir in the chilies. Adjust the seasoning, if necessary, and add extra chili paste, tamarind paste, and soy sauce, if desired.

3. The sauce can be served hot or at room temperature, or let it cool completely and store in an airtight container in the refrigerator for up to one week.

NACHO SAUCE

MAKES: about 1¼ cups	**PREP TIME:** 5 mins	**COOK TIME:** 15 mins

THIS CREAMY NACHO SAUCE GETS ITS HEAT FROM DRY MUSTARD, HOT SAUCE, AND FINELY CHOPPED CHILIES. YOU CAN DIP TORTILLA CHIPS IN THE SAUCE, MIX IT WITH COOKED PASTA, OR TOP A BAKED POTATO WITH A SPOONFUL.

INGREDIENTS

1 cup shredded sharp cheddar cheese

3 tbsp cornstarch

1 tbsp dry mustard

1 cup milk

2 tbsp cream cheese

2 tsp sriracha or other hot chili sauce

2 red or green jalapeños, finely chopped

salt and pepper (optional)

1. Mix together the cheddar cheese, cornstarch, and dry mustard in a heatproof bowl, then set aside.

2. Put the milk into a saucepan and bring just to a boil. Stir ¼ cup of the hot milk into the cheese mixture, stirring until well blended. Add the cheese mixture to the remaining milk, whisking vigorously.

3. Bring the mixture back just to a boil, then reduce the heat and simmer, whisking frequently, for 5 minutes, until the sauce is smooth and has reduced. Remove the pan from the heat and stir in the cream cheese and chili sauce. Season with salt and pepper, if using, then stir in the chilies.

4. The sauce can be used immediately, or let it cool completely and stored in an airtight container in the refrigerator for up to three days. To serve, reheat gently without boiling.

TIP
DO NOT ADD THE CORNSTARCH OR DRY MUSTARD DIRECTLY TO THE HOT MILK OR LUMPS WILL FORM. WHISK TO BE SURE OF A SMOOTH MIXTURE.

DANGEROUS ADOBO SAUCE

MAKES: about 1¼ cups	**PREP TIME:** 10 mins	**COOK TIME:** 1½–1¾ hrs

CHIPOTLE CHILIES ARE DRIED JALAPEÑOS, WHICH ARE AVAILABLE IN TWO FORMS, MORITA OR MECO. MECO CHIPOTLES GIVE A SMOKIER FLAVOR THAT WORKS WELL WITH SLOW-COOKED MEAT DISHES.

INGREDIENTS
¼ cup tomato paste

2½ cups water

⅓ cup white wine vinegar

12 dried chipotle chilies, stems removed

4 garlic cloves, crushed

½ red onion, minced

2 tbsp packed light brown sugar

1 tbsp ground cumin

1 tbsp dried Mexican oregano or dried thyme

2 tsp hot smoked paprika

2 tsp cayenne pepper

½ tsp salt

pepper (optional)

1. Dissolve the tomato paste in the water and vinegar in a deep saucepan. Stir in the other ingredients and season with pepper, if using. Cover and bring to a boil.

2. Uncover, reduce the heat to low, and simmer for 1¼–1½ hours, or until the chilies are soft and the sauce thickens.

3. Transfer the sauce to a blender or food processor and puree. Strain the sauce through a strainer into a bowl, rubbing back and forth with a wooden spoon and scraping the bottom of the strainer to produce as much sauce as possible. Set aside to cool completely.

4. The sauce can be used immediately, or stored in an airtight container in the refrigerator for up to three weeks.

MEATBALLS IN ADOBO SAUCE

SERVES: 4	PREP TIME: 20 mins	COOK TIME: 30–35 mins

WHEN YOU'RE EXPECTING CHILI LOVERS FOR DINNER, THIS IS A WONDERFUL QUICK-AND-EASY DISH TO SERVE. THE SAUCE IS SPICY HOT, AND ANY LEFTOVERS WILL MAKE A GREAT TACO FILLING.

INGREDIENTS

⅓ cup dried bread crumbs

3–4 tbsp milk

3 tbsp all-purpose flour, for dusting

8 oz ground round beef

8 oz lean ground pork

4 large garlic cloves, finely chopped

2 eggs, beaten

3 tbsp finely chopped fresh parsley or cilantro

1 tsp ground cinnamon

1 tsp sweet paprika

¼ cup sunflower oil, for frying, plus extra if needed

1¼ cups Dangerous Adobo Sauce (see page 101)

1 cup coarsely shredded mozzarella cheese

¼ cup shredded cheddar cheese

salt and pepper (optional)

1. Combine the bread crumbs and milk in a bowl and let soak for 10 minutes. Put the flour on a plate and set aside. Preheat the oven to 400°F.

2. Combine the beef, pork, garlic, eggs, parsley, cinnamon, and paprika with the bread crumb mixture in a large bowl. Season with salt and pepper, if using, and stir to combine.

3. Using wet hands, shape the mixture into 24 equal balls. Heat the oil in a large skillet over medium heat. Working in batches, lightly roll the meatballs in the flour, shaking off the excess. Add the meatballs to the pan and cook, turning, until brown all over, then transfer to a baking dish.

4. Pour the Adobo Sauce over the meatballs in the dish, then sprinkle with the mozzarella cheese and cheddar cheese. Bake in the preheated oven for 15–20 minutes, or until the meatballs are cooked through, the sauce is hot, and the cheese is melting.

5. If cheese has not browned after when the meatballs are done, preheat the broiler to high. Place the dish under the broiler and brown for 2–3 minutes.

VEGETABLE MAINS & SIDES

This chapter focuses on fiery vegetable dishes.
Eggplant, zucchini, butternut squash, and celery root
are all livened up with smoky spices and hot chilies. Our
selection ranges from Celery Root, Fennel & Peach Slaw
and Gratin of Green Chilies to Sweet Potato & Broccoli
Burgers and Smoky Barbecue Beans.

EGGPLANT
STUFFED WITH
BULGUR WHEAT

SERVES: 4	PREP TIME: 35 mins	COOK TIME: 55 mins

A GOOD SOURCE OF VITAMINS, MINERALS, AND FIBER, EGGPLANTS WORK WELL WITH SPICES IN THIS WHOLESOME DISH. FIBER-RICH BULGUR WHEAT PROVIDES THE BASE FOR THE HERBACEOUS VEGETABLE STUFFING.

INGREDIENTS

1 tsp ground cumin

1 tsp ground coriander

1 tsp paprika

1 tsp crushed red pepper flakes

2 tbsp olive oil

2 eggplant, cut in half lengthwise

1 red onion, coarsely chopped

2 garlic cloves, chopped

1 cup fine bulgur wheat

1 cup vegetable broth or stock

3 tbsp coarsely chopped fresh cilantro

3 tbsp coarsely chopped fresh mint

1 cup crumbled feta cheese

⅓ cup slivered almonds, toasted

1½ tbsp lemon juice

2 tsp pomegranate molasses

salt and pepper (optional)

TO GARNISH

1 tbsp chopped fresh mint

1 tsp pomegranate molasses,

½ cup plain Greek yogurt

¼ cup pomegranate arils

1. Preheat the oven to 350°F. Mix the cumin, ground coriander, paprika, crushed red pepper flakes, and 1½ tablespoons of olive oil in a small bowl. Use a sharp knife to slice the eggplant flesh in a diagonal, crisscross pattern, without piercing the skin. Drizzle the cumin mixture over the eggplant, allowing it to sink into the cuts. Place the eggplant halves on a baking sheet and roast in the oven for 35 minutes.

2. Meanwhile, heat the remaining 1½ teaspoons of olive oil in a large skillet over medium heat. Add the onion and garlic and sauté for 3–4 minutes, or until softened. Reduce the heat to medium–low, add the bulgur wheat, and stir well. Reduce the heat to low, pour in the vegetable broth or stock, and stir until the liquid has been absorbed. Remove the mixture from the pan and transfer to a large bowl.

3. Remove the eggplant from the oven and let rest for 10 minutes. Keep the oven on. Using a tablespoon, scoop out the center of the eggplant, leaving a clear edge to support the filling.

4. Add the eggplant flesh to the bulgur mixture. Stir in the fresh cilantro, mint, feta, almonds, lemon juice, and pomegranate molasses. Stir well and season with salt and pepper, if using.

5. Divide the stuffing among the eggplant halves and return to the oven for 15 minutes. Serve immediately, garnished with the fresh mint, molasses, yogurt, and pomegranate arils.

SPICED VEGETABLE & HALLOUMI SKEWERS

SERVES: 8	PREP TIME: 25 mins	COOK TIME: 30 mins

THESE SPICED SKEWERS MAKE A GREAT VEGETARIAN OPTION FOR BARBECUES AND, SIMPLE TO MAKE, THEY ARE PERFECT FOR A CROWD. YOU WILL NEED 16 WOODEN SKEWERS FOR THIS RECIPE.

INGREDIENTS

8 oz cremini mushrooms, halved or quartered depending on size

8 oz halloumi, cut into ½-inch chunks

1 large eggplant, cut into ¾-inch chunks

3 cups cherry tomatoes

1 tbsp ras el hanout

1 tsp sea salt flakes

3 tbsp olive oil

pinch of sea salt flakes

1. Preheat the oven to 350°F. Soak 16 wooden skewers in water for 20 minutes, then drain well.

2. Put the mushrooms, cheese, eggplant, and cherry tomatoes in a large bowl and toss well. Add the ras el hanout, 1 teaspoon of salt, and the oil and toss again.

3. Thread the vegetables and cheese onto the skewers in any order, then place them on two large baking pans. Roast for 30 minutes, or until the vegetables are tender. Sprinkle with a large pinch of salt and serve two skewers per person.

TIP
IF YOU WANT, ASSEMBLE THE SKEWERS IN ADVANCE AND LET THEM MARINATE FOR A FEW HOURS IN THE REFRIGERATOR BEFORE COOKING.

RED KIDNEY BEAN STEW

| SERVES: 4 | PREP TIME: 20 mins | COOK TIME: 30–35 mins |

HIGH IN FIBER, THIS DELICIOUS NORTHERN INDIAN DISH OF SPICED RED KIDNEY BEANS IS BEST SERVED WITH RICE AND WARM FLATBREADS. IT CAN EASILY BE MADE A DAY AHEAD—SIMPLY REHEAT IT AND SERVE WITH THE YOGURT.

INGREDIENTS

2 tbsp vegetable oil or peanut oil

2 tsp cumin seeds

2 onions, finely chopped

2 tsp grated fresh ginger

6 garlic cloves, crushed

2 fresh green chilies, finely chopped

2 large tomatoes, coarsely chopped

2 tsp ground coriander

1 tsp ground cumin

¼ tsp ground turmeric

1 tsp garam masala

1 (29 oz) can red kidney beans, drained and rinsed

1 tsp palm sugar or brown sugar

2 cups warm water

1 tsp salt

¼ cup finely chopped fresh cilantro, to garnish

2 tbsp plain yogurt, to serve

1. Heat the oil in a large saucepan and add the cumin seeds. When they stop crackling, add the onions and sauté until soft.

2. Add the ginger and garlic and sauté for 2 minutes. Add the chilies, tomatoes, ground coriander, cumin, turmeric, and garam masala and stir-fry for 12–15 minutes.

3. Add the red kidney beans, sugar, water, and salt and cook for 10–12 minutes, or until the beans are soft.

4. Remove from the heat and transfer to a serving dish. Garnish with the chopped cilantro and serve with yogurt.

TIP CANNED BEANS ARE USED IN THIS RECIPE FOR SPEED. IF USING DRIED BEANS, COOK ACCORDING TO THE PACKAGE DIRECTIONS BEFORE USING.

BENGALI
VEGETABLE STEW

SERVES: 4	PREP TIME: 30 mins, plus standing	COOK TIME: 30–35 mins

THIS TRADITIONAL BENGALI VEGETABLE STEW USES A MIXTURE OF CHOPPED VEGETABLES AND IS COOKED WITH A MUSTARD SEED AND WHITE POPPY SEED PASTE. PANCH PHORON IS A BENGALI SPICE MIXTURE MADE OF FENUGREEK SEEDS, FENNEL SEEDS, MUSTARD SEEDS, NIGELLA SEEDS, AND CUMIN SEEDS.

INGREDIENTS

⅓ cup plus 2 tsp white poppy seeds

3 tbsp black mustard seeds

2 tsp grated fresh ginger

¼ cup vegetable oil or peanut oil

2 fresh green chilies, halved lengthwise

1 tbsp panch phoron (Indian five-spice blend)

2 small fresh bitter melons (kerala), cut into ½-inch cubes

2 potatoes, peeled and cut into ½-inch cubes

1 eggplant, cut into ½-inch cubes

1 zucchini, cut into ½-inch cubes

1 carrot, cut into ½-inch cubes

1 tomato, finely chopped

⅔ cup fresh or frozen peas

1¾ cups cold water

¼ tsp ground turmeric

2 tsp salt

1 tsp palm sugar or brown sugar

½ cup milk

1. Soak the white poppy seeds and 2 tablespoons of the mustard seeds in warm water for 1 hour. Drain and blend with the ginger to make a paste.

2. Heat the oil in a large skillet and add the remaining mustard seeds and the chilies. When the mustard seeds start to pop, add the panch phoron and all the vegetables. Add half the water and stir to mix well, then cover tightly and cook, stirring frequently, over medium heat for 10–12 minutes.

3. Add half the white poppy seed and mustard seed paste, the turmeric, and salt. Add the remaining water and cook, stirring frequently, over low–medium heat for an additional 10–15 minutes.

4. Add the remaining white poppy seed and mustard seed paste, the sugar, and milk, and cook for an additional 5 minutes, or until the vegetables are tender. Serve hot.

1 2
3

SPICY COUSCOUS WITH NUTS, DATES & APRICOTS

SERVES: 4	PREP TIME: 15 mins	COOK TIME: 15 mins

COUSCOUS COMBINED WITH DRIED FRUIT AND NUTS IS DELICIOUS SERVED WITH GRILLED MEATS AND SPICY STEWS. TRADITIONALLY, A FRUITY COUSCOUS WOULD ALSO BE DUSTED WITH CINNAMON AND SERVED ON ITS OWN, OFTEN AS A PALATE CLEANSER.

INGREDIENTS

2 cups couscous

1¾ cups boiling water

½ tsp sea salt flakes

2 tbsp olive oil

1–2 tbsp clarified butter or butter

large pinch of saffron

1 cup blanched almonds

1 cup unsalted pistachios

1–2 tsp ras el hanout

¾ cup thinly sliced dates

¾ cup thinly sliced dried apricots

2 tsp ground cinnamon, to garnish

1. Put the couscous into a shallow heatproof bowl. Put the boiling water into a heatproof bowl, stir in the salt, then pour it over the couscous, cover, and let stand for 10 minutes.

2. Drizzle the oil over the couscous. Using your fingers, rub it into the grains to break up the lumps.

3. Heat the butter in a heavy skillet over medium heat. Add the saffron, almonds, and pistachios and cook for 1–2 minutes or until the nuts begin to brown and emit a nutty aroma, stirring occasionally. Stir in the ras el hanout, toss in the dates and dried apricots, and cook, stirring, for 2 minutes. Fluff up the couscous using a fork, then transfer to the pan, mix well, and heat through. Remove from the heat.

4. Pile the couscous onto a serving plate in a mound. Sprinkle the cinnamon through your fingers to create vertical lines from the top of the mound to the bottom, like the spokes of a wheel. Serve immediately.

GRATIN OF GREEN CHILIES WITH CREAM & CHEESE

| SERVES: 4–6 | PREP TIME: 20–25 mins, plus 10 mins standing | COOK TIME: 25 mins |

THE TRULY DELICIOUS COMBINATION OF PEPPERY, LEMONY CHILIES AND SWEET, RICH CREAM OFFERS THE PERFECT BALANCE OF TEXTURE AND FLAVOR.

INGREDIENTS
1½ lbs thin-fleshed, mild green chilies, preferably Anaheim

1 cup light cream

1 cup heavy cream

1½ cups crumbled feta cheese or queso fresco

salt and pepper (optional)

soft cornmeal tortillas, to serve

1. Wipe the chilies, but don't remove the stems or seeds. Using tongs, hold the chilies over a gas flame, or cook under a preheated broiler or oven on the highest setting, until the skins are black and blistered in places. Transfer to a covered bowl and let stand for 10 minutes to loosen the skins. Remove the skins. Slice the flesh into ribbons and arrange in a gratin dish.

2. Meanwhile, heat all the cream in a small saucepan and remove it as soon as it reaches boiling point. Pour it over the chili ribbons and sprinkle with the cheese. Season with a little salt and pepper—not too much, because the cheese may already be salty and one or two of the chilies may be hot.

3. Preheat the broiler to high. Cook the mixture for 8–10 minutes, or until brown and bubbling. Meanwhile, wrap the tortillas in aluminum foil and warm through in a preheated low oven for 5 minutes. Serve the gratin piping hot with warm tortillas.

SWEET POTATO & BROCCOLI BURGERS

| MAKES: 4–6 | PREP TIME: 10–12 mins, plus 1 hr chilling | COOK TIME: 45–50 mins |

THERE ARE A LOT OF INTERESTING TEXTURES AND FLAVORS VYING FOR YOUR ATTENTION IN THESE TASTY VEGETARIAN BURGERS.

INGREDIENTS

3 sweet potatoes, peeled and cut into chunks

2½ cups broccoli florets

2–3 garlic cloves, crushed

1 red onion, finely chopped or grated

1½–2 fresh red jalapeños, deseeded and finely chopped

1½ cups shredded halloumi cheese or queso fresco cheese

2 tbsp whole wheat flour

2–3 tbsp sunflower oil

3 onions, sliced

1 tbsp chopped fresh cilantro

salt and pepper (optional)

1. Bring a saucepan of lightly salted water to a boil, add the sweet potatoes, bring back to a boil, and cook for 15–20 minutes, or until tender. Drain and mash. Bring a separate small saucepan of lightly salted water to a boil, add the broccoli, bring back to a boil, and cook for 3 minutes, then drain and plunge into cold water. Drain again, then add to the mashed sweet potato.

2. Stir in the garlic, red onion, chilies, cheese, and salt and pepper, if using. Mix well and shape into four to six equal patties, then coat in the flour. Cover and let chill in the refrigerator for at least 1 hour.

3. Heat 1½ tablespoons of the oil in a heavy skillet. Add the sliced onions and sauté over medium heat for 12–15 minutes, or until soft. Stir in the cilantro and reserve.

4. Preheat the grill or broiler. Brush the patties with the remaining oil and cook over medium heat for 5–6 minutes on each side, or until cooked through.

5. Top the burgers with the reserved fried onions and cilantro and serve immediately.

VEGETABLE CHILI

SERVES: 4	PREP TIME: 35 mins	COOK TIME: 1 hr 20 mins

THIS DELICIOUS, SPICY VEGETARIAN CHILI IS FULL OF VEGETABLES, BEANS, AND WONDERFUL FLAVORS. YOU CAN INCREASE THE AMOUNT OF CHILI POWDER AND CUMIN IF YOU WANT TO INCREASE THE HEAT FACTOR.

INGREDIENTS

1 eggplant, cut into 1-inch slices

2 tbsp olive oil

1 large red onion, finely chopped

2 red or yellow bell peppers, deseeded and finely chopped

3–4 garlic cloves, finely chopped

1 (28 oz) can diced tomatoes

1 tbsp mild chili powder

½ tsp ground cumin

½ tsp dried oregano

2 small zucchini, quartered lengthwise and sliced

1 (15 oz) can kidney beans, drained and rinsed

2 cups water

1 tbsp tomato paste

6 scallions, finely chopped

1 cup shredded cheddar cheese, for sprinkling

salt and pepper (optional)

1. Brush the eggplant slices on one side with oil. Heat half the remaining oil in a large, heavy skillet over medium–high heat. Add the eggplant slices, oiled side up, and cook for 5–6 minutes, or until brown on one side. Turn the slices over, cook on the other side until brown, and transfer to a plate. Cut into bite-size pieces.

2. Heat the remaining oil in a large saucepan over medium heat. Add the onion and red bell peppers and cook, stirring occasionally, for 3–4 minutes, or until the onion is soft but not brown.

3. Add the garlic and cook for an additional 2–3 minutes, or until the onion is beginning to brown.

4. Add the tomatoes, chili powder, cumin, and oregano. Season with salt and pepper, if using. Bring just to a boil, reduce the heat, cover, and simmer gently for 15 minutes.

5. Add the zucchini, eggplant pieces, and beans. Stir in the water and the tomato paste. Bring back to a boil, then cover and continue simmering for 45 minutes, or until the vegetables are tender. Add salt and pepper, if using. Ladle into serving bowls, top with the scallions, and sprinkle with the cheese. Serve.

CHILI SAUCES
AROUND THE WORLD

Although chilies originated in South and Central America, they are now grown in just about every part of the world—and are a key part of the many hot and spicy flavors associated with particular regions.

South America

The home of the chili produces a traditionally mild cuisine—so the addition of a sauce is often needed to add a little fire, although even the hot sauces tend to focus on flavor rather than heat. The most popular remains adobo sauce, made from chilies such as chipotle, with Mexican oregano, onions, and tomatoes, but all amateur chefs will have their own recipe, often using chipotle or jalapeños.

United States of America

Our hot sauces are made with chilies, vinegar, and salt, and often with the addition of fruits and vegetables as diverse as raspberries, mangoes, tomatoes, and carrots to mellow out the flavor or to thicken the sauce. The most popular chilies used in American sauces are jalapeño, chipotle, habanero, and cayenne, and the results range from very mild barbecue sauces to the spicy hot pepper sauce.

Caribbean

Sauces made from chilies feature heavily in Caribbean cuisine and, like their American cousins, most are made with the addition of fruit and vegetables to temper the flavor. However, most Caribbean sauces feature habanero and Scotch bonnet chilies, so the results still tend to be much hotter. Homemade sauces are common, with onions and garlic often added for extra piquancy.

Europe

Believe it or not, two of the hottest chili sauces in the world originate from Great Britain. Made from

the naga viper and infinity chilies, they remain a specialized taste. However, the Portuguese peri-peri sauce, made from crushed peri-peri chilies with lime, citrus peel, garlic, and various herbs, remains popular across the continent.

Middle East

The ancients of this region believed that chilies held near-magical healing powers, and so much of the traditional cuisine features sauces with chilies as ingredients. The most popular remains harissa—made from fresh and dried hot chilies blended into a thick paste with garlic, olive oil, and spices, such as caraway seeds. Other examples are shatta, used in Levantine cuisine, made with chilies and olive oil, and skhug from Yemen and Israel.

Asia

Chili sauces are used widely in Asia. Often made with the addition of beans, many sauces are made as a thick paste, which can be added to curries or stews, used as a dipping sauce, or used for stir-frying. India is one of the largest chili producers and they define the experience of many of the dishes. Specific Asian sauces include the Chinese Lao Gan Ma, combining chilies with soybean paste, and the Korean gochujang, made with chili, glutinous rice, fermented soybeans, and salt. Thailand is known for its sriracha sauce as well as its spicy dipping sauces (nam chim) and fish sauces (nam pla). Sambal is a chili sauce from Indonesia, Malaysia, and Sri Lanka that has developed an international appeal.

BUTTERNUT SQUASH LINGUINE WITH ARRABBIATA SAUCE

SERVES: 2	PREP TIME: 15 mins	COOK TIME: 20 mins

PASTA IS A MUCH-LOVED STAPLE, BUT OCCASIONALLY IT'S GREAT TO TRY SOMETHING DIFFERENT. VEGETABLES PREPARED SO THEY LOOK A LOT LIKE SPAGHETTI TASTE GREAT, AND THEY ARE ALSO LOW IN CARBS.

INGREDIENTS

1 butternut squash

cooking oil spray, for greasing

2 tbsp chopped fresh flat-leaf parsley, to garnish

ARRABBIATA SAUCE
1 tbsp olive oil

1 onion, chopped

2 garlic cloves, crushed

1 red chili, deseeded and finely chopped

3 tbsp red wine

1 tsp sugar

1 tsp crushed red pepper flakes

2 tsp red pesto

¾ cup canned chopped tomatoes

4 anchovy fillets from a jar, drained

8 black olives, pitted and coarsely chopped

1 tsp dried Italian seasoning

½ tsp salt

½ tsp pepper

1. Cut the bulbous end off the squash and set aside for another recipe. Cut the stem off the squash and discard. Peel the remaining squash. If you are using a spiralizer, cut the squash into two chunks and put each chunk through the spiralizer. If you are using a julienne peeler, set the squash on a stable work surface and slice off julienne strips.

2. To make the arrabbiata sauce, put a large saucepan over medium–low heat and add the oil. Add the onion and sauté for 8 minutes, or until soft and transparent. Add the garlic and chili and stir for 1 minute. Add the wine, sugar, crushed red pepper flakes, pesto, tomatoes, anchovies, olives, Italian seasoning, salt, and pepper and simmer for 20 minutes.

3. Meanwhile, preheat the oven to 375°F. Put the julienned squash spaghetti on a large baking pan and spray with the cooking oil. Bake in the preheated oven for 6 minutes, and then turn the squash over using tongs. Bake for an additional 4 minutes, or until the strands are just tender with the occasional tinge of gold.

4. Transfer the squash to two warm serving plates. Spoon the arrabbiata sauce on top, garnish with the parsley, and serve immediately.

1 2
3

CELERY ROOT, FENNEL & PEACH SLAW

SERVES: 4	PREP TIME: 10 mins	COOK TIME: none

A GOOD SLAW, THIS ONE SPICED UP WITH SRIRACHA SAUCE, CAN BE USED IN MANY WAYS: AS A QUICK SNACK, AS A SANDWICH OR WRAP COMPONENT, OR SERVED WITH COLD MEAT AND A CRISPY SALAD.

INGREDIENTS

¼ cup mayonnaise

1 tsp sriracha sauce

1 tsp horseradish sauce

zest and juice of 1 lemon

½ tsp pepper

2 ripe peaches, pitted and thinly sliced

⅓ celery root, cut into matchsticks

1 fennel bulb, sliced

1 small red onion, sliced

1. In a large bowl, whisk together the mayonnaise, sauce, horseradish sauce, lemon zest and juice, and pepper.

2. Add the peaches, celery root, fennel, and onion to the bowl.

3. Mix well to combine thoroughly, then serve immediately.

TIP
THIS SLAW WILL WORK WELL WITH ANY STONE FRUIT AND IS GREAT SERVED WITH PORK, CHICKEN, OR FISH.

SMOKY BBQ
BEANS

SERVES: 4	PREP TIME: 10 mins	COOK TIME: 30 mins

THE CANNELLINI BEANS IN THIS RECIPE ARE INFUSED WITH DEEP-SEATED, SMOKY FLAVORS, AND THE FINAL DISH COMBINES THESE TENDER, CREAMY BEANS WITH AN ADDICTIVE BARBECUE FLAVOR.

INGREDIENTS

¼ cup olive oil

1 large onion, chopped

2 garlic cloves, chopped

2 celery stalks, chopped

1 large carrot, chopped

1 tsp fennel seeds

2 tsp dried oregano

2 tsp smoked paprika

1 tbsp chipotle chili paste

1 tbsp molasses

2 cups tomato puree or tomato sauce

1 (15 oz) can cannellini beans, drained and rinsed

salt and pepper (optional)

1. Heat the oil in a large saucepan over medium heat. Add the onion, garlic, celery, and carrot, cover with a lid, and let cook for 15 minutes, or until translucent and soft.

2. Add the fennel seeds, oregano, paprika, chili paste, and molasses. Cook for 5 minutes, until the sugars start to caramelize.

3. Add the tomato puree or sauce and beans and cook for an additional 10 minutes.

4. Season with salt and pepper, if using, and serve.

TIP
FOR THE CARNIVORE IN YOUR LIFE, TRY ADDING CHOPPED SMOKED BACON, CHORIZO, OR SLICED HOT DOGS TO THE BEANS.

SPICY MASHED EGGPLANT

SERVES: 4	PREP TIME: 15–20 mins	COOK TIME: 45–55 mins

THIS VERSION OF BAINGAN KA BHARTA HAS ITS ORIGINS IN THE PUNJAB. BHARTAS ARE LARGELY NORTH INDIAN IN ORIGIN AND CAN BE MADE FROM ALL KINDS OF VEGETABLES.

INGREDIENTS

4 large eggplant

2 tbsp vegetable oil or peanut oil

4 tbsp butter

2 onions, finely chopped

2 tsp grated fresh ginger

4 garlic cloves, crushed

2 fresh green chilies, finely sliced

3 tomatoes, finely chopped

2 tsp salt

1 tsp chili powder

1 tsp smoked paprika

2 tsp ground coriander

1 tsp ground cumin

1 tsp ground turmeric

½ tsp garam masala

⅓ cup finely chopped fresh cilantro

1. Pierce each eggplant all over with a fork and roast them over an open flame (if you have a gas stove-top) or under a medium-hot broiler, turning them from time to time, for 20–25 minutes, until the skin blackens and chars. To check if an eggplant is cooked, press the back of a spoon into the skin; if it enters the eggplant as it would soft butter, the eggplant is done. Let cool.

2. When the eggplant are cool enough to handle, remove the skins and coarsely mash the pulp. Set aside.

3. Heat the oil and butter in a large, nonstick skillet and add the onions. Sauté for 5–6 minutes, until soft. Add the ginger, garlic, and chilies, and stir-fry for 1–2 minutes.

4. Stir in the tomatoes and salt, and cook for 12–15 minutes. Add the chili powder, paprika, ground coriander, cumin, and turmeric.

5. Stir in the reserved eggplant and cook for 3–4 minutes. Stir in the garam masala and fresh cilantro. Serve immediately.

THAI RED FRIES

| SERVES: 4 | PREP TIME: 15 mins | COOK TIME: 30 mins |

THESE UNUSUAL OVEN-BAKED FRIES HAVE AN EXPLOSION OF FLAVORS—THEY'RE SWEET, SPICY, TANGY, SALTY, AND ALL-AROUND DELICIOUS.

INGREDIENTS

3 tbsp vegetable oil

2 tbsp packed light brown sugar

2 tbsp Thai fish sauce

2 tbsp lime juice

1 tbsp Thai red curry paste

½ tsp cayenne pepper

8 white potatoes (about 2 pounds)

CILANTRO KETCHUP

1 garlic clove

⅓ cup fresh cilantro

1 cup ketchup

2 tbsp lime juice

1. Preheat the oven to 450°F. Grease a large baking sheet with 1 tablespoon of the oil.

2. Put the remaining oil, sugar, fish sauce, lime juice, curry paste, and cayenne pepper into a mixing bowl and stir together until well combined.

3. Peel the potatoes, if desired, and cut them into ¼ x ¼-inch sticks. Add them to the mixture in the bowl and toss to coat. Let stand for about 5 minutes, then, using a slotted spoon, transfer the potatoes to the prepared baking sheet, letting the excess marinade run off into the bowl. Spread the potatoes in a single layer. Bake in the preheated oven for 25–30 minutes, turning after about 15 minutes, until brown and crisp.

4. Meanwhile, to make the ketchup, chop the garlic and cilantro in a food processor. Add the ketchup and lime juice and process until well combined. Transfer to a serving bowl.

5. Serve the fries hot with the ketchup for dipping.

MEAT & POULTRY MAINS

When it's a sizzling, spice-packed meaty main that's needed, these dishes won't disappoint. Choose from chicken, turkey, beef, pork, or lamb, and impress your family and friends with Goan Spiced Chicken; Hot Sesame Beef; Turkey Stir-Fry with Spiced Coffee Glaze; Pork with Chilies, Vinegar & Garlic; or treat yourself to a Colossal Lamb Kabob with Hot Chili Sauce.

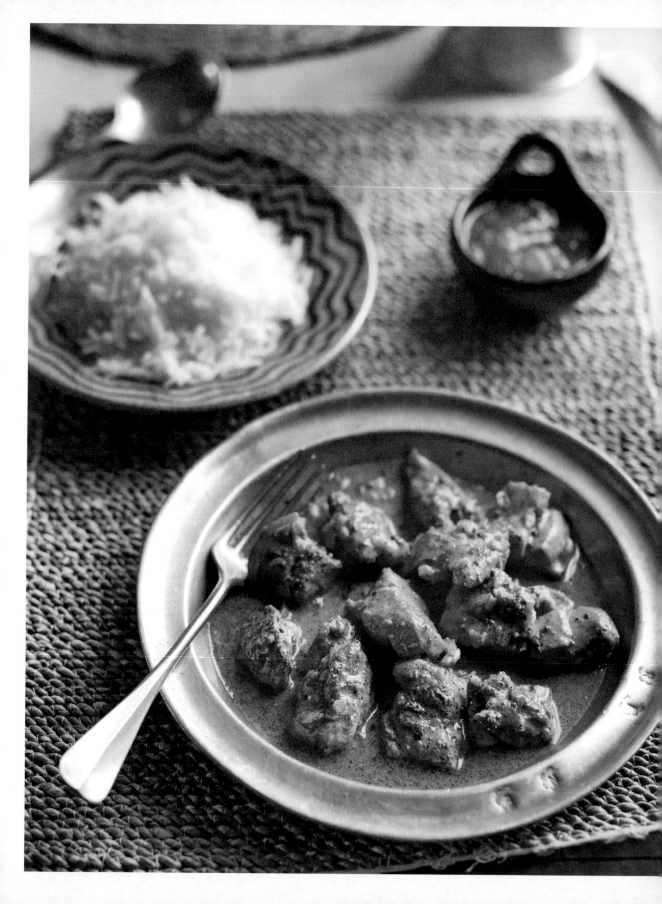

GOAN
SPICED CHICKEN

| **SERVES:** 4 | **PREP TIME:** 20 mins | **COOK TIME:** 35–40 mins |

THIS CLASSIC, SPICY CHICKEN DISH FROM THE SHORES OF GOA IS A LOCAL FAVORITE. MADE FROM A BLEND OF COCONUT MILK, RED CHILIES, AND AROMATIC SPICES, IT IS BEST SERVED WITH STEAMED RICE AND MANGO CHUTNEY.

INGREDIENTS

6 black peppercorns

3 cloves

2 tsp fennel seeds

4 dried red chilies

1 tsp cardamom seeds

2 tsp white poppy seeds

2 cinnamon sticks

2 tsp salt

1 tsp ground turmeric

1 tsp ground cumin

1 tsp ground coriander

¼ cup vegetable oil or peanut oil

1 onion, minced

3 garlic cloves, crushed

1¼ pounds boneless, skinless chicken thighs, cut into bite-size pieces

1¾ cups coconut milk

1¼ cups cold water

1 tsp tamarind paste

1. Put a large, nonstick skillet over medium heat and add the peppercorns, cloves, fennel seeds, dried red chilies, cardamom seeds, white poppy seeds, and cinnamon sticks. Dry-fry for 1–2 minutes, then remove from the heat and let cool.

2. Put the cooled whole spices into a spice grinder with the salt, turmeric, cumin, and ground coriander. Process until ground to a fairly fine powder.

3. Heat the oil in a large saucepan, add the onion and garlic, and sauté over medium heat for 2–3 minutes. Increase the heat to high, add the chicken, and stir-fry for 5–6 minutes, or until sealed.

4. Add the spice mixture and stir-fry for 1–2 minutes, then add the coconut milk and water. Bring to a boil, then reduce the heat to low–medium and simmer gently for 15–20 minutes. Stir in the tamarind paste and cook for an additional 2–3 minutes, or until the chicken is cooked through and tender, with no sign of pink when the thickest part is pierced with the tip of a sharp knife. Serve immediately.

SPICY HAMBURGERS WITH GUACAMOLE & POTATO WEDGES

SERVES: 4	PREP TIME: 1 hr	COOK TIME: 45 mins

A GOOD HAMBURGER IS HARD TO BEAT, AND IF YOU MAKE YOUR OWN, YOU'LL KNOW WHAT IS IN IT AND YOU CAN CONTROL THE PERCENTAGE OF FAT.

INGREDIENTS

1 lb sirloin steak, visible fat removed, diced

½ tsp chili powder

2 tsp cumin seeds, coarsely crushed

1 tbsp fresh thyme leaves

4 Russet potatoes, unpeeled, scrubbed, and cut into wedges

3 tbsp extra-virgin olive oil

1 tsp paprika

sea salt and pepper (optional)

GUACAMOLE

1 large avocado, pitted and peeled

juice of 1 lime

2 scallions, finely chopped

TO SERVE

4 spelt burger buns, halved

1 romaine lettuce heart, shredded

handful of arugula leaves

2 large tomatoes, sliced

1. Preheat the oven to 400°F. With the motor running on a food processor, drop in a few pieces of steak at a time, until it is all coarsely chopped. Alternatively, press the pieces through a grinder on the coarse setting.

2. Put the chili powder, half the cumin seeds, half the thyme, and a little salt and pepper, if using, in a bowl and mix well. Rub the mixture into the steak, then shape the mixture into four patties. Cover and chill in the refrigerator for 15 minutes.

3. Bring a saucepan of water to a boil, add the potato wedges, and cook for 4–5 minutes. Drain well and transfer to a roasting pan. Drizzle the wedges with 2 tablespoons of oil, then turn them until they are well coated. Sprinkle with the paprika, the remaining cumin and thyme, and a little salt and pepper, if using. Bake, turning once, for 25–30 minutes, or until golden brown.

4. For the guacamole, put the avocado into a shallow bowl and mash with a fork. Add the lime juice and scallions, season with a little salt and pepper, if using, and mix well.

5. Preheat the broiler to medium–high. Brush the burgers with a little of the remaining oil, then cook, turning halfway through, for 8–10 minutes, or a little less for those who like their burgers pink in the middle. Let stand for a few minutes. Meanwhile, toast the buns, then stack the lettuce, arugula, tomatoes, hot patties, and a spoonful of guacamole on the bottoms and add the bun tops. Serve with the potato wedges.

TURKEY STIR-FRY WITH SPICED COFFEE GLAZE

SERVES: 4	PREP TIME: 25 mins, plus 1 hr marinating	COOK TIME: 15 mins

THIS TEMPTING, FLAVORFUL STIR-FRY REQUIRES ONLY FIFTEEN MINUTES OF COOKING, AND IT WILL UNDOUBTEDLY SPICE UP YOUR DAY.

INGREDIENTS

1 lb turkey breast, sliced into thin strips

1 tsp finely grated fresh ginger

2 garlic cloves, crushed

1 tsp Chinese five-spice paste

4 tsp sesame oil

¼ cup strong black coffee, cooled

¼ cup teriyaki sauce

2 tbsp honey

2 tbsp rice wine vinegar

2 tsp cornstarch

6 scallions, trimmed and sliced

1 red bell pepper, deseeded and thinly sliced

1 yellow bell pepper, deseeded and thinly sliced

salt and pepper (optional)

1 lb cooked egg noodles, to serve

1. Put the turkey in a shallow, bowl and add the ginger, garlic, Chinese five-spice paste, and half the oil. Stir well, then cover and let marinate at room temperature for 1 hour.

2. Mix together the coffee, teriyaki sauce, honey, vinegar, and cornstarch in a small bowl. Cover and set aside.

3. Heat the remaining oil in a large wok until almost smoking. Remove the turkey from the marinade, add to the wok, and stir-fry over high heat for 3–4 minutes, until brown. Add the scallions, red bell pepper, and yellow bell pepper and stir-fry for an additional 1–2 minutes.

4. Pour in the coffee mixture and stir-fry for an additional 1–2 minutes, until the sauce has thickened and coated the turkey and vegetables. Serve with the noodles.

HOT SESAME BEEF

SERVES: 4	PREP TIME: 20 mins	COOK TIME: 10 mins

THIS SESAME BEEF IS BEAUTIFULLY SUCCULENT AND STICKY, WITH THE BEEF AND VEGETABLES BATHED IN A SPICY SAUCE OF BEEF BROTH, SOY SAUCE, GINGER, GARLIC, AND CRUSHED RED PEPPER FLAKES.

INGREDIENTS

1 lb tenderloin steak, cut into thin strips

1½ tbsp sesame seeds

½ cup beef broth or stock

2 tbsp soy sauce

2 tbsp grated fresh ginger

2 garlic cloves, finely chopped

1 tsp cornstarch

½ tsp crushed red pepper flakes

3 tbsp sesame oil

1 large head of broccoli, cut into florets

1 yellow bell pepper, deseeded and thinly sliced

1 fresh red chili, finely sliced

1 tbsp chili oil, or to taste

cooked white rice, to serve

1. Mix the beef strips with 1 tablespoon of the sesame seeds in a small bowl.

2. In a separate bowl, stir together the broth or stock, soy sauce, ginger, garlic, cornstarch, and red pepper flakes.

3. Heat 1 tablespoon of the sesame oil in a large wok. Add the beef strips and stir-fry for 2–3 minutes. Remove and set aside, then wipe out the wok with paper towels.

4. Heat the remaining sesame oil in the wok, add the broccoli, yellow bell pepper, red chili, and chili oil and stir-fry for 2–3 minutes.

5. Stir in the broth mixture, cover, and simmer for 2 minutes.

6. Return the beef to the wok and simmer until the juices thicken, stirring occasionally. Cook for an additional 1–2 minutes. Sprinkle with the remaining sesame seeds and serve over wild rice.

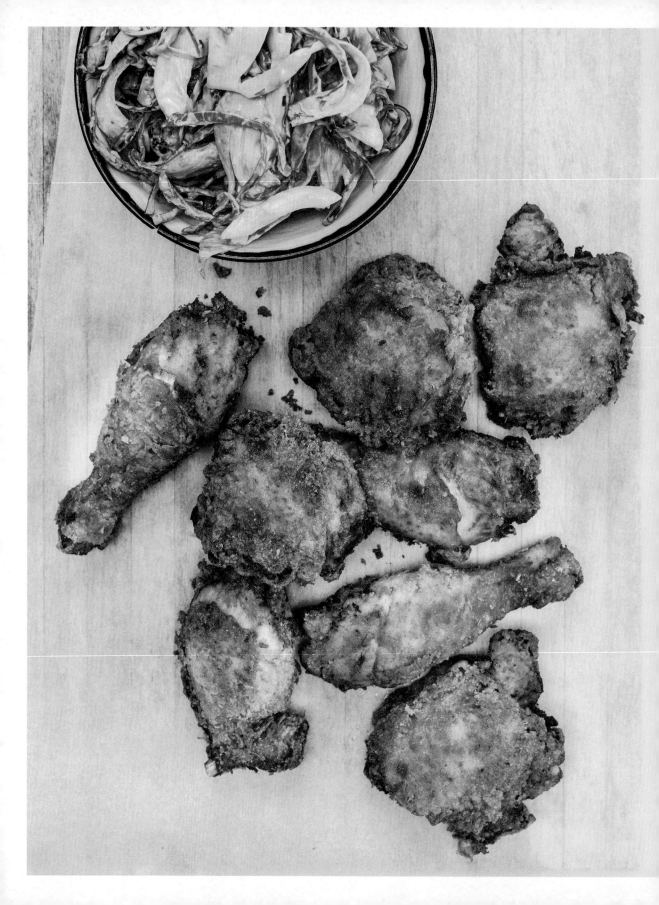

SPICY FRIED CHICKEN WITH RED CABBAGE & CHILI COLESLAW

| SERVES: 4 | PREP TIME: 20 mins, plus 2–3 hrs marinating | COOK TIME: 35 mins |

INSTEAD OF THE USUAL BREAD CRUMBS, THIS CHICKEN HAS A CRUNCHY COATING OF CORNMEAL, QUINOA FLOUR, AND WHOLE-WHEAT FLOUR, WHICH WORKS EXCELLENTLY WITH THE ZINGY FLAVORS OF THE COLESLAW.

INGREDIENTS

1 cup sour cream

½ tsp cayenne pepper

1 garlic clove, crushed

4 chicken thighs and 4 chicken drumsticks (about 1¾ lbs)

2 tsp coarse cornmeal

2 tbsp quinoa flour

2 tbsp whole wheat flour

vegetable oil, for deep-frying

sea salt and pepper (optional)

COLESLAW

2 cups shredded red cabbage

4 cups shredded fennel

1 red chili, deseeded and thinly sliced lengthwise

½ cup plain Greek yogurt

juice of ¼ lemon

1. Put the sour cream, cayenne, and garlic into a large bowl and season well with salt and pepper, if using. Add the chicken and toss well. Cover the bowl with plastic wrap and marinate in the refrigerator for 2–3 hours, or overnight if you have time.

2. To make the coleslaw, put all the ingredients into a large bowl and toss well, then season with salt and pepper, if using. Cover and chill in the refrigerator.

3. Mix together the cornmeal and flours on a plate and season with salt and pepper, if using. Heat a heavy skillet filled halfway with oil over medium–high heat to 350°F, or until a cube of bread browns in 30 seconds. While it heats, sprinkle the flour mixture over the chicken.

4. Cook the chicken in two batches, because too much chicken in the pan will make the oil temperature drop. Using tongs, carefully place half the chicken in the oil. Cook for 6–8 minutes, then turn and cook for an additional 6–8 minutes, until the coating is a deep golden brown, the chicken is cooked through to the bone, and the juices run clear with no sign of pink when the tip of a sharp knife is inserted into the thickest part of the meat.

5. Using a slotted spoon, transfer the cooked chicken to paper towels to drain, then keep warm in a low oven while you cook the second batch.

6. Serve the chicken on with the coleslaw.

THAI GREEN CHICKEN CURRY & UDON NOODLES

SERVES: 4	PREP TIME: 10 mins	COOK TIME: 15 mins

THAI GREEN CURRY IS SO CHRISTENED BECAUSE OF THE GREEN CHILIES FROM WHICH IT IS PREPARED—GREEN CURRY PASTE IS USED IN THIS FRAGRANT, CREAMY CURRY, AND YOU CAN CALM DOWN OR ACCENTUATE THE HEAT TO YOUR TASTE.

INGREDIENTS

1 tbsp vegetable oil

1 shallot, diced

1–3 tsp Thai green curry paste

1 (13½ -oz) can coconut milk

1 tbsp Thai fish sauce

juice of 1 lime

1 tbsp packed light brown sugar

⅔ cup fresh basil leaves

⅔ cup fresh cilantro leaves

1 pound fresh udon noodles

2⅓ cups shredded cooked chicken

3 scallions, thinly sliced, to garnish

1. Heat the oil in a nonstick skillet over medium heat. Add the shallot and cook for 5 minutes, until soft. Add the curry paste and cook, stirring, for 1 minute.

2. Scoop off the thick cream in the can that will have risen to the top of the coconut milk. Add the cream to the pan with the fish sauce, lime juice, and sugar. Cook, stirring frequently, for 1–2 minutes. Stir in the remaining coconut milk and bring the mixture to a boil. Reduce the heat to low and simmer, stirring occasionally, for an additional 5 minutes, or until the sauce thickens. Remove from the heat and let cool slightly.

3. Transfer the mixture to a food processor, add the basil and cilantro, and process until smooth and bright green. Return the sauce to the pan and reheat over medium–low heat.

4. Cook the noodles according to the package directions and place them in a large serving bowl.

5. Add the chicken and sauce to the noodles and toss to combine. Serve immediately, garnished with the scallions.

2 4
5

WHOLE TANDOORI CHICKEN

SERVES: 4 | **PREP TIME:** 35 mins, plus 24 hrs marinating | **COOK TIME:** 55 mins

THIS DISH ORIGINATES IN THE PUNJAB. THE "TANDOORI" IN THE NAME COMES FROM THE TANDOOR, A CYLINDRICAL CLAY OVEN, WHERE THIS CHICKEN DISH IS TRADITIONALLY PREPARED AT AN EXTREMELY HIGH TEMPERATURE.

INGREDIENTS

1 (3¼ lb) chicken

2 tsp garam masala

1¼ cups plain yogurt

1 onion, finely chopped

2 garlic cloves, crushed

1-inch piece fresh ginger, peeled and grated

juice of 1 lemon

2 tbsp tomato paste

1 tsp chili powder

1 tsp ground cumin

1 tsp ground turmeric

1 tbsp paprika (not smoked)

1 tsp salt

TO SERVE
basmati rice

naan or other flatbread

lime wedges

hot lime pickle (available in specialty sores)

1. Cut two slits into each chicken leg and two into each thigh. The cuts should just reach the bone. Make two shallower cuts into the fleshiest part of each breast. These are to let the marinade penetrate into the meat.

2. Mix all of the remaining ingredients together in a food processor and blend to a smooth paste. Put the chicken into a large dish and cover it in the paste, massaging it deep into the skin and flesh. Place the chicken, uncovered, in the refrigerator to marinate for as long as possible—preferably 24 hours.

3. Remove the chicken from the refrigerator before cooking to bring it to room temperature. Preheat the oven to 425°F. Put the chicken into the oven and cook, uncovered, for 20 minutes, then reduce the heat to 350°F. Baste the chicken and cook for another 35 minutes. When fully cooked the juices will run clear when the tip of a sharp knife is inserted into the thickest part of the meat. Turn off the oven and open the door, but keep the chicken inside to rest for 20 minutes. Serve with rice, naan, lime wedges, and lime pickle.

SPICY RICE WITH CHICKEN & POMEGRANATE

| SERVES: 4 | PREP TIME: 25 mins | COOK TIME: 1 hr |

SPICE UP YOUR LUNCH WITH THIS TEMPTING CHICKEN-AND-RICE DISH, FINISHED WITH JUICY, PINK POMEGRANATE ARILS, WHICH PACK A POWERFUL NUTRIENT PUNCH, PLUS VIVID, GREEN, ANTIOXIDANT-RICH FRESH HERBS.

INGREDIENTS

4 large chicken thighs

2 tsp Chinese five-spice powder

2 tbsp olive oil

2 red onions, finely sliced

2 garlic cloves, finely sliced

5 cardamom pods, crushed

2 star anise

1¼ cups brown rice

3 cups vegetable broth or stock

⅔ cup coarsely chopped fresh mint

½ cup coarsely chopped fresh flat-leaf parsley

1 cup pomegranate arils

¼ cup toasted almond silvers

finely grated zest and juice of 1 lemon

salt and pepper (optional)

1. Preheat the oven to 400°F. Put the chicken thighs onto a baking pan and sprinkle with the Chinese five-spice powder. Drizzle with 1 tablespoon of olive oil and roast in the preheated oven for 20 minutes, or until the juices run clear when the thickest part of the meat is pierced and no traces of pink remain in the center. Remove from the oven and set aside to cool.

2. Meanwhile, heat the remaining tablespoon of olive oil in a large saucepan over medium–low heat. Add the onion and gently sauté for 10–12 minutes, or until soft and starting to caramelize. Stir in the garlic, cardamom pods, and star anise and cook for an additional minute. Add the rice and stir well.

3. Pour in the broth or stock and bring the pan to a boil. Cover and simmer gently for 25–30 minutes, or until all the broth has been absorbed and the rice is tender.

4. Once the chicken is cool enough to handle, remove the meat from the bones and finely slice. Add to the rice mixture, with any remaining juices, and season with salt and pepper, if using.

5. Stir in half of the mint and parsley. Top with the remaining herbs, pomegranate arils, toasted almonds, lemon juice, and zest and serve immediately.

SPICES FROM
DRIED FRUITS & SEEDS

Spices are made from aromatic plants, such as seeds, fruits, vegetables, or roots, and are used to season food. Chili is classed as a spice, but there are many others from which to choose.

The spice trade was a significant driving force within the world economy starting toward the end of the Middle Ages, with the most common and popular spices in the medieval period including black pepper (the most expensive), cinnamon, cumin, nutmeg, ginger, and cloves. Spices can be created from different plant forms—from dried fruits or seeds, such as mustard, nutmeg, fennel, and black pepper; arils, such as mace; barks, such as cassia and cinnamon; dried flower buds, such as cloves; stigmas, such as saffron; and roots, such as turmeric and ginger. Here, we look at spices that are sourced from dried fruits or seeds.

Allspice, also called pimento, is an aromatic spice created from the dried unripe berry of the West Indian allspice tree. It was called "allspice" because it was felt to capture the flavors of cinnamon, nutmeg, and cloves. It is used widely in Caribbean cuisine, especially in jerk seasoning, and in mole sauces.

Black pepper is the dried fruit of a flowering vine in the Piperaceae family, and peppercorns are a familiar feature in every kitchen. First grown in southern India, it is commonly used to enhance the appetite and give dishes a warming quality.

Cayenne pepper is from the chili family, and the dried fruit is commonly used in its powdered form after the peppers are dried, ground, and sifted to create the powder that gives heat to spicy dishes.

Cumin seeds are small seeds, similar in size to rice grains, taken from the plant Cuminum cyminum. They have a warm and slightly bitter quality and are used widely in South Asian, North African, and Latin American cuisines. Cumin is available in whole and ground form.

Fennel is a dried, oval-shaped seed that comes from the herb Foeniculum vulgare, which is distinctive for its licorice flavor (see opposite, top right). Fennel seeds can be brown or green—green seeds are the best choice for cooking.

Mustard seeds are the fruit pods of the mustard plant and are available as black, brown, yellow, or white seeds. They have a nutty taste and are used extensively in Indian cooking.

Nutmeg is the seed of the nutmeg tree, Myristica fragrans (see opposite, bottom), which is indigenous to the Spice Islands in Indonesia. It has a comforting spicy warmth and is usually used in powdered form. It is equally useful in sweet and savory dishes.

Paprika originated in central Mexico and is made from the air-dried fruits of the chili pepper, which are then formed into a powder. Bright red, it is often used to add color to dishes. It is available in different strengths but is milder than cayenne pepper and has a sweet quality.

Star anise is the dried fruit of an evergreen tree called Illicium velum that is native to southwest China (see opposite, top left). It has a distinctive eight-point star shape and contains anethole, an oil with a licorice flavor. It is widely used in Chinese and Indian cuisine.

MEXICAN TURKEY BURGERS

| SERVES: 4 | PREP TIME: 25 mins, plus 1 hr chilling | COOK TIME: 20 mins |

THESE DELICIOUS ROAST BURGERS ARE IDEAL FOR A COOKOUT OR CAN EASILY BE PREPARED IN THE KITCHEN TO GIVE A BARBECUE FLAVOR TO AN INDOOR MEAL.

INGREDIENTS

1 lb ground fresh turkey

¾ cup canned refried beans

2–4 garlic cloves, crushed

1–2 fresh jalapeños, deseeded and finely chopped

2 tbsp tomato paste

1 tbsp chopped fresh cilantro

1 tbsp sunflower oil

salt and pepper, to taste

shredded baby spinach

TO SERVE

4 cheese-topped burger buns, halved

salsa

guacamole

tortilla chips

1. Put the ground turkey in a bowl and break up any large lumps. Beat the refried beans until smooth, then add them to the turkey in the bowl.

2. Add the garlic, chilies, tomato paste, and cilantro with salt and pepper to taste and mix together. Shape into four equal patties, then cover and let chill in the refrigerator for 1 hour.

3. Preheat the grill, if using. Otherwise, add the oil to a large skillet over medium–high heat, until hot. Add the patties and cook for 5–6 minutes on each side, or until browned and cooked through. If grilling, brush the patties with the oil and cook over medium-hot coals for 5–6 minutes on each side, or until cooked through.

4. Place the spinach on the bottom halves of the burger buns and top with the burgers. Spoon over a little salsa and guacamole and add the top of the bun. Serve immediately with tortilla chips on the side.

SPICED TURKEY STEW WITH WHOLE GRAIN COUSCOUS

SERVES: 4	PREP TIME: 20 mins	COOK TIME: 25 mins

CAPTURE THE FLAVORS OF MIDDLE EASTERN COOKING WITH THIS EASY, LIGHTLY SPICED STOVE-TOP TURKEY STEW.

INGREDIENTS

1 tbsp virgin olive oil

1 lb boneless, skinless turkey breast, cut into ¾-inch pieces

1 onion, coarsely chopped

2 garlic cloves, finely chopped

1 red bell pepper, deseeded and coarsely chopped

1 orange pepper, deseeded and coarsely chopped

4 tomatoes, coarsely chopped

1 tsp cumin seeds, coarsely crushed

1 tsp paprika

zest and juice of 1 lemon

sea salt and pepper (optional)

TO SERVE

1⅓ cups whole grain Israeli couscous or pearl couscous

2 tbsp coarsely chopped fresh flat-leaf parsley

2 tbsp coarsely chopped fresh cilantro

1. Heat the oil in a large skillet over medium heat. Add the turkey, a few pieces at a time, then add the onion. Sauté, stirring, for 5 minutes, or until the turkey is golden.

2. Add the garlic, red and orange bell peppers, and tomatoes, then stir in the cumin seeds and paprika. Add the lemon juice and season with salt and pepper, if using. Stir well, then cover and cook, stirring from time to time, for 20 minutes, or until the tomatoes have formed a thick sauce and the turkey is cooked through and the juices run clear with no sign of pink when a piece is cut in half.

3. Meanwhile, fill a saucepan halfway with water and bring to a boil. Add the couscous and cook according to the package directions, or until just tender. Transfer to a strainer and drain well.

4. Spoon the couscous onto plates and top with the turkey stew. Mix the parsley and cilantro with the lemon zest, then sprinkle with the stew and serve.

PORK WITH CHILIES, VINEGAR & GARLIC

| SERVES: 4 | PREP TIME: 10 mins, plus 30–40 mins marinating | COOK TIME: 1¼–1½ hrs |

WHEN THE PORTUGUESE TRAVELED TO INDIA, THEY TOOK PORK PRESERVED IN VINEGAR, GARLIC, AND PEPPER, WHICH WAS SPICED TO SUIT INDIAN TASTES. THUS, THIS VINDALOO DISH WAS BORN.

INGREDIENTS

2–6 dried red chilies, torn

5 cloves

1-inch piece cinnamon stick, broken up

4 green cardamom pods

½ tsp black peppercorns

½ mace blade

¼ nutmeg, grated

1 tsp cumin seeds

1½ tsp coriander seeds

½ tsp fenugreek seeds or yellow mustard seeds

2 tsp garlic paste

1 tbsp ginger paste

3 tbsp apple cider vinegar or white wine vinegar

1 tbsp tamarind juice or juice of ½ lime

1½ lbs boneless leg of pork, cut into 1-inch cubes

¼ cup vegetable oil or peanut oil, plus 2 tsp

2 large onions, finely chopped

1¼ cups warm water

1 tsp salt, or to taste

1 tsp packed dark brown sugar

2 large garlic cloves, finely sliced

8–10 fresh curry leaves

1. Grind the first ten ingredients (all the spices) to a fine powder in a spice grinder. Transfer the ground spices to a bowl and add the garlic and ginger pastes, vinegar, and tamarind juice. Mix together to form a paste.

2. Put the pork into a large bowl and rub about one-quarter of the spice paste into the meat. Cover and let marinate in the refrigerator for 30–40 minutes.

3. Heat the ¼ cup of oil in a heavy saucepan over medium heat, add the onions, and cook, stirring frequently, for 8–10 minutes, until lightly browned. Add the remaining spice paste and cook, stirring constantly, for 5–6 minutes. Add 2 tablespoons of the water and cook until it evaporates. Repeat with another 2 tablespoons of water.

4. Add the marinated pork and cook over medium–high heat for 5–6 minutes. Add the salt, sugar, and the remaining water. Bring to a boil, then reduce the heat to low, cover, and simmer for 50–55 minutes.

5. Meanwhile, heat the 2 teaspoons of oil in a small saucepan over low heat. Add the sliced garlic and cook, stirring, until it begins to brown. Add the curry leaves and let sizzle for 15–20 seconds. Stir the garlic mixture into the pan. Serve immediately.

RIB OF BEEF WITH A HOT HORSERADISH CRUST

| SERVES: 4–6 | PREP TIME: 10 mins | COOK TIME: 60 mins, plus 30 mins resting |

A SPICY COATING OF CREAMED HORSERADISH AND MUSTARD MAKES THIS SUCCULENT RIB INTO SOMETHING EXTRA SPECIAL. CARVE IT FOR DINNER AND ANY LEFTOVERS WILL BE DELICIOUS SERVED COLD.

INGREDIENTS

4½ lbs beef ribs

1 tsp salt

1 tsp pepper

¼ cup olive oil

HORSERADISH CRUST

2 tbsp extra virgin olive oil

¼ cup creamed horseradish

2 tbsp English or spicy brown mustard

zest and juice of 1 lemon

½ tsp salt

½ tsp pepper

1. Preheat the oven to 350°F.

2. Place the beef ribs on a large cutting board and season with salt and pepper.

3. Put all of the horseradish crust ingredients into a small bowl and mix until combined to a coarse paste.

4. Heat the olive oil in a large skillet over medium–high heat and sear the ribs on all sides. Transfer to a wire rack positioned over a roasting pan and brush all over with the horseradish paste. Put the pan into the preheated oven and cook for 50 minutes.

5. Remove the ribs from the oven and set aside to rest for about 30 minutes before serving. Serve with the juices from the roasting pan poured over the top.

COLOSSAL LAMB KABOB WITH HOT CHILI SAUCE

| SERVES: 1 | PREP TIME: 10 mins | COOK TIME: 10 mins |

THESE SPICY HOT LAMB KABOBS ARE TRULY SIMPLE YET SERIOUSLY FILLING. PERFECT FOR THE BARBECUE OR FOR A SOLO EVENING MEAL, THE KABOB AND CHILI SAUCE CAN ALSO BE SERVED WITH WARM PITA BREAD.

INGREDIENTS

1 lb leg of lamb, diced

2 tbsp olive oil

1 tsp dried thyme

1 tsp paprika

1 tsp ground cumin

1 large flatbread

1 small red onion, sliced

1 tomato, chopped

small bunch of fresh cilantro, chopped

½ lemon

salt and pepper, to taste

sriracha or other hot chili sauce and plain yogurt, to serve

1. In a medium bowl, mix the lamb with the olive oil, thyme, and spices and season with salt and pepper.

2. Preheat a large ridged grill pan or grill.

3. Thread the lamb onto two large metal skewers, and cook in the preheated pan for 4–5 minutes on each side, or until cooked to your liking.

4. Heat a large, dry skillet and cook the flatbread for a few seconds on both sides until soft.

5. Remove the lamb from the skewers, place on the flatbread, and top with the onion, tomato, and cilantro. Squeeze the lemon on top and serve immediately with the sriracha and plain yogurt.

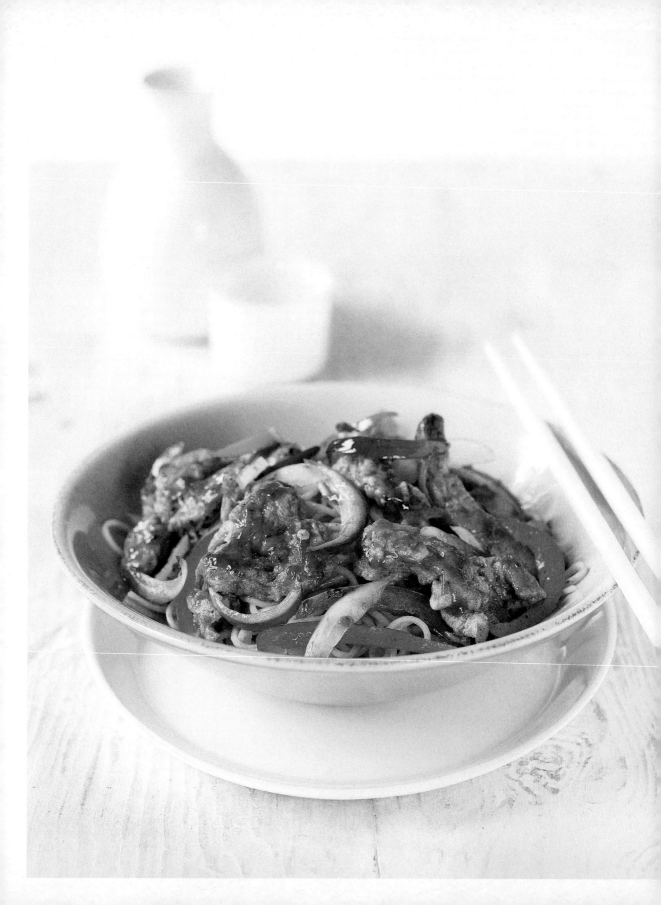

LAMB WITH
BLACK BEAN SAUCE

SERVES: 4	PREP TIME: 25 mins	COOK TIME: 12–14 mins

CHINESE FIVE-SPICE POWDER AND BLACK BEAN SAUCE CREATE SOME MAGIC WITH LAMB AND BELL PEPPERS TO GIVE THIS DISH PLENTY OF WARMTH AND PIZAZZ.

INGREDIENTS

1 lb boneless lamb shoulder or boneless lamb chops

1 egg white, lightly beaten

¼ cup cornstarch

1 tsp Chinese five-spice powder

3 tbsp sunflower oil

1 red onion, sliced

1 red bell pepper, deseeded and sliced

1 green bell pepper, deseeded and sliced

1 yellow or orange bell pepper, deseeded and sliced

⅓ cup douchi black bean sauce

freshly cooked noodles, to serve

1. Using a sharp knife, slice the lamb into thin strips.

2. Mix together the egg white, cornstarch, and Chinese five-spice powder. Toss the lamb strips in the mixture until evenly coated.

3. Heat the oil in a preheated wok or large skillet and cook the lamb over high heat, stirring, for 5 minutes, or until it crisps around the edges.

4. Add the onion and bell pepper slices to the wok and stir-fry for 5–6 minutes, or until the vegetables just begin to soften.

5. Stir the black bean sauce into the lamb mixture in the wok and heat through.

6. Transfer the lamb and sauce to warm serving plates and serve hot with freshly cooked noodles of your choice.

TIP
DOUCHI BLACK BEAN SAUCE IS MADE WITH SALTY FERMENTED BEANS. CHECK THE FINISHED DISH FOR FLAVOR BEFORE ADDING ANY EXTRA SALT.

FISH & SEAFOOD MAINS

When you're in the mood for a taste of the sea, these zingy fish dishes will deliver a spicy punch of flavors to satisfy your cravings. Including shrimp, crawfish, scallops, and sardines, the succulent recipes feature Maharashtrian Salmon in a Sauce, Shrimp & Chili-Lime Spaghetti, Whole Spice-Crusted Red Snapper, and Crawfish Cakes with Mashed Avocado & Chili.

MAHARASHTRIAN
SALMON IN A SAUCE

SERVES: 4	PREP TIME: 5–10 mins	COOK TIME: 15–20 mins

THIS SIMPLE FISH DISH IS PACKED WITH FLAVOR. YOU CAN USE ANY FIRM FISH FILLET OR STEAKS INSTEAD OF THE SALMON, IF DESIRED. SERVE WITH FRESHLY COOKED RICE TO SOAK UP THE DELICIOUS COOKING LIQUID.

INGREDIENTS

⅓ cup vegetable or peanut oil

8 (5½ oz) salmon steaks

2 tsp cornstarch

1 tsp hot chili powder

1 tsp paprika

½ tsp ground turmeric

2 tsp ground cumin

1 tsp ground coriander

2 tsp salt

1 tsp tamarind paste

1¾ cups coconut milk

1¾ cups cold water

freshly cooked rice, to serve

1. Heat the oil in a nonstick saucepan and add the fish. Cook for 1–2 minutes on each side.

2. Mix together the cornstarch, spices, salt, tamarind paste, and coconut milk. Pour this mixture into the saucepan with the water.

3. Bring to a boil, then reduce the heat, cover, and cook gently for 10–12 minutes, or until the fish is cooked through and the sauce has thickened slightly (it should still be runny). Serve immediately with rice.

SPICED BAKED COD WITH HARISSA & PINE NUT CRUST & ROAST CHERRY TOMATOES

SERVES: 2	PREP TIME: 10 mins	COOK TIME: 15 mins

THIS DISH IS INCREDIBLY QUICK TO PREPARE, AND MAKES A DELICIOUS, EASY MIDWEEK MEAL. THE SPICY, CRUNCHY TOPPING IS A WONDERFUL CONTRAST FOR THE SOFT FISH FLAKES.

INGREDIENTS
¼ cup pine nuts

⅓ cup fresh bread crumbs

grated zest of 1 lemon

2 tbsp coarsely chopped fresh cilantro

pinch of sea salt

1 tsp olive oil

20 cherry tomatoes (still on the vine)

2 (7 oz) cod fillets

2 tsp rose harissa

1. Preheat the oven to 400°F. Crush the pine nuts in a mortar and pestle. Transfer them to a bowl, add the bread crumbs, lemon zest, cilantro, salt, and oil, and mix well.

2. Put the cherry tomatoes onto a large baking pan and add the cod fillets, skin side down, arranging everything in a single layer. Spread a teaspoon of rose harissa over each cod fillet, then top with the bread crumb mixture, pressing down gently.

3. Bake on a high shelf in the oven for 15 minutes, or until the topping is crisp and golden and the fish flakes easily when pressed with a knife. Serve the cod hot with the tomatoes.

TIP
SUBSTITUTE RED SNAPPER, HALIBUT, OR ANY OTHER FIRM WHITE FISH FOR THE COD—WHATEVER IS THE FRESHEST AND BEST VALUE OF THE DAY.

MOROCCAN FISH SOUP

| SERVES: 4 | PREP TIME: 20 mins | COOK TIME: 55 mins–1¼ hrs |

PREPARED WITH RED SNAPPER, THIS SOUP IS FULL OF RICH FLAVORS AND SPICY WARMTH PRODUCED BY THE RICH COMBINATION OF SPICES.

INGREDIENTS
2 tbsp olive oil

1 large onion, finely chopped

pinch of saffron

½ tsp ground cinnamon

1 tsp ground coriander

½ tsp ground cumin

½ tsp ground turmeric

¾ cup canned diced tomatoes

1¼ cups fish broth or stock

4 small red snapper steaks

½ cup pitted green olives

1 tbsp chopped preserved lemon

3 tbsp chopped fresh cilantro

salt and pepper (optional)

couscous, to serve

1. Heat the oil in a flameproof casserole dish. Add the onion and cook over low heat, stirring occasionally, for 10 minutes, or until soft but not browned. Add the saffron, cinnamon, ground coriander, cumin, and turmeric and cook the mixture for an additional 30 seconds, stirring constantly.

2. Add the tomatoes and fish broth or stock and stir well. Bring to a boil, reduce the heat, cover, and simmer for 15 minutes. Uncover and simmer for 20–35 minutes, or until thickened.

3. Cut each red snapper in half, then add the fish pieces to the casserole, pushing them down into the liquid. Simmer the stew for an additional 5–6 minutes, or until the fish is just cooked.

4. Carefully stir in the olives, preserved lemon, and chopped cilantro. Season with salt and pepper, if using, and serve with couscous.

SHRIMP & CHILI-LIME SPAGHETTI

| SERVES: 4 | PREP TIME: 20–30 mins | COOK TIME: 30 mins |

THIS DISH, COMBINING PLUMP, JUICY SHRIMP, ZUCCHINI, AND SPAGHETTI WITH THE ADDED BITE OF JALAPEÑOS, PROVIDES AN EASY MEAL.

INGREDIENTS

- 1–2 tsp salt
- 1 lb dried spaghetti
- 4 garlic cloves, crushed
- 2–4 red or green jalapeños, deseeded and diced
- 4 small zucchini, diced
- 3 scallions, thinly sliced
- 2 tbsp olive oil
- 1 lb peeled and deveined raw shrimp
- finely grated zest and juice of 1 lime
- 2 tbsp butter
- salt (optional)

1. Add the salt to a large saucepan of water and bring to a boil, add the spaghetti, bring back to a boil, and cook for 8–10 minutes, or according to package directions, until tender but still firm to the bite.

2. Drain the pasta in a colander and set aside until needed. Return the pan to the heat, add the oil, and heat over medium–high heat. Add the garlic and cook, stirring, for 1–2 minutes, until it begins to soften. Add the chilies, zucchini, and salt, if using, and cook, stirring occasionally, until the zucchini begins to brown.

3. Add the shrimp and lime juice and zest to the pan. Add the scallions and cook, stirring occasionally, until the shrimp are pink and cooked through. Add the butter and reserved spaghetti and cook, stirring, for 1–2 minutes, until most of the liquid has evaporated. Serve immediately.

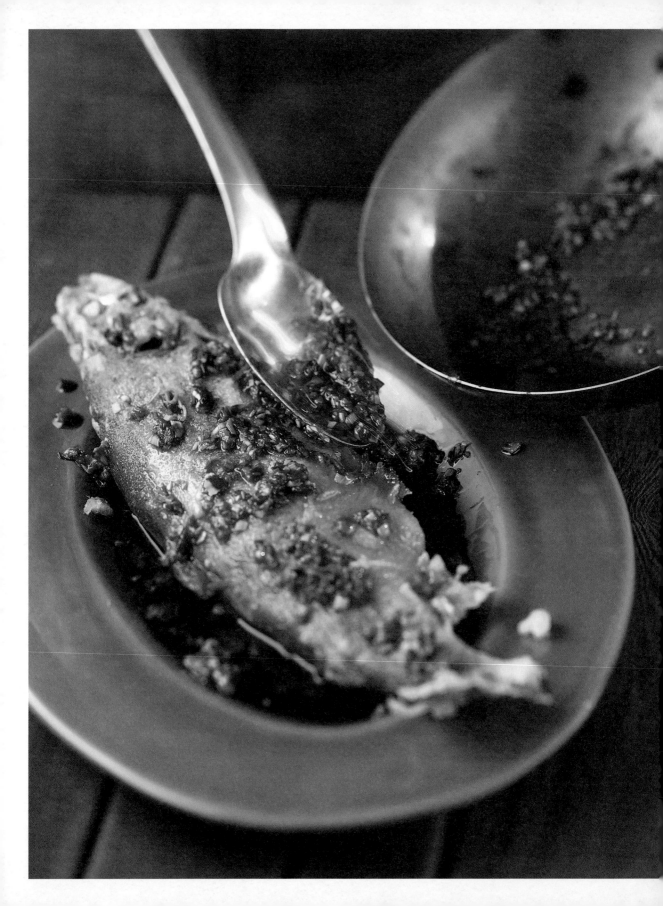

DEEP-FRIED FISH WITH CHILI BEAN SAUCE

SERVES: 4–6	PREP TIME: 25 mins	COOK TIME: 20–25 mins

DEEP-FRIED FRESHWATER FISH WITH A TEMPTING SAUCE THAT COMBINES THE FLAVORS OF CHILI, GARLIC, GINGER, AND CHILI BEAN OFFERS UP A DIVINE TREAT WITH SOMETHING OF A KICK.

INGREDIENTS

4 whole freshwater fish, such as trout or carp (about 1 lb), gutted

1 tbsp all-purpose flour

pinch of salt

⅓ cup water

vegetable oil or peanut oil, for deep-frying

SAUCE

⅓ cup vegetable oil or peanut oil

1 tsp crushed red pepper flakes

1 garlic clove, finely chopped

1 tsp finely chopped fresh ginger

1 tbsp chili bean sauce

½ tsp white pepper

2 tsp sugar

1 tbsp white rice vinegar

1 tsp finely chopped scallion

1. To prepare the fish, clean and dry thoroughly. Mix together the flour, salt, and water to create a light batter. Coat the fish.

2. Heat enough oil for deep-frying in a wok, deep fryer, or large heavy saucepan to 350–375°F, or until a cube of bread browns in 30 seconds. Deep-fry the fish until the skin is crisp and golden brown. Drain, set aside, and keep warm.

3. To make the sauce, first heat all but 1 tablespoon of the oil in a small saucepan and, when smoking, pour in the red pepper flakes. Remove from heat and set aside.

4. In a preheated wok or deep saucepan, heat the remaining oil and stir-fry the garlic and ginger until fragrant. Stir in the chili bean sauce, then add the oil and pepper flake mixture. Season with the pepper, sugar, and vinegar. Turn off the heat and stir in the scallion. Pour the sauce over the fish and serve immediately.

FISH IN TOMATO & CHILI SAUCE
WITH FRIED ONIONS

| **SERVES:** 4 | **PREP TIME:** 10 mins, plus 15–20 mins marinating | **COOK TIME:** 35–40 mins |

FIRM-FLESHED FISH IS PAN-FRIED UNTIL BROWNED AND THEN SIMMERED IN AN ALLURINGLY SPICED CHILI-AND-TOMATO SAUCE. THIS DISH IS BEST SERVED WITH FRESHLY COOKED RICE AND POPADAMS.

INGREDIENTS

1½ pounds white fish fillets, such as halibut, cod, or red snapper, cut into 5-cm/2-inch pieces

2 tbsp lemon juice

1 tsp salt, or to taste

1 tsp ground turmeric

¼ cup vegetable oil or peanut oil, plus extra for pan-frying

2 tsp sugar

1 large onion, finely chopped

2 tsp ginger paste

2 tsp garlic paste

½ tsp ground fennel seeds

1 tsp ground coriander

½–1 tsp chili powder

⅔ cup canned diced tomatoes

1¼ cups warm water

2–3 tbsp chopped fresh cilantro

freshly cooked rice, to serve

popadams, to serve

1. Place the fish on a large plate and gently rub in the lemon juice, ½ teaspoon of the salt, and ½ teaspoon of the turmeric. Set aside for 15–20 minutes.

2. Pour enough oil into a skillet to fill to a depth of about ½ inch and place over medium–high heat. When the oil is hot, cook the pieces of fish, in a single layer, until well browned on both sides and a light crust is formed. Drain on paper towels.

3. Heat the ¼ cup of oil in a saucepan or skillet over medium heat and add the sugar. Let it brown, watching it carefully because once it browns, it will blacken quickly. As soon as the sugar is brown, add the onion and cook for 5 minutes, until soft. Add the ginger and garlic pastes and cook for an additional 3–4 minutes, or until the mixture begins to brown.

4. Add the ground fennel seeds, ground coriander, chili powder, and the remaining turmeric. Cook for about a minute, then add half the tomatoes. Stir and cook until the tomato juice has evaporated, then add the remaining tomatoes. Continue to cook, stirring, until the oil separates from the spice paste.

5. Pour in the water and add the remaining salt. Bring to a boil and reduce the heat to medium. Add the fish, stir gently ,and reduce the heat to low. Cook, uncovered, for 5–6 minutes, then stir in half the chopped cilantro and remove from the heat. Garnish with the remaining cilantro and serve immediately.

GROW YOUR OWN CHILIES

We know you love the taste of chilies, but did you realize they're easy to grow yourself? It is not necessary to live in a hot country or near the equator—with some care, anyone can nurture a crop.

The good news for aspiring chili growers is that you don't need a yard—chilies grow best in flowerpots, even a hanging basket or inside on a windowsill, so just a little amount of outdoor space is enough.

1. Sow seeds indoors six to eight weeks before the last expected frost. Wait until nighttime temperatures stay above 55°F before moving the plants outdoors.

2. Fill a seed module flat with seed-starting mix, lightly water, and place a seed in each cell or compartment of the tray. Put some more seed-starting mix on top. Water again, cover with plastic wrap, and put somewhere warm. Check them every day and keep the plants moist.

3. After a month you should see sprouts coming through. Remove the plastic wrap and move to a warm windowsill. Keep moist.

4. When your seedlings sprout a second set of leaves, carefully transplant to small flowerpots (see opposite, top left), and encourage growth with a weekly tomato fertilizer.

5. At about 5 inches tall, transplant to bigger pots. Support any drooping plants by tying them to a stake, as their roots are shallow. In hot weather, plant outdoors in full sun in a soil enriched with organic matter that is moisture retentive and drains well.

6. Try not to let your plants grow above 12 inches tall—if you pinch the tops above the leaves, you will encourage bushiness and more flowers.

7. As the plants develop, flowers will start to appear on your plants.

8. Start giving the plants a liquid fertilizer once the flowers appear, or just before they start to form, and carry on until the chilies have been harvested. Fertilize the plants every two weeks.

9. After flowering, the flowers will turn brown and drop off. This is normal and indicates that a chili is pushing its way through the flower. Keep the plant fertilized and watered as the chilies ripen.

10. Harvest your chili peppers by removing them from plants with a sharp knife or pruners to prevent any damage to the plant. Snip off (and eat) the first crop while they're still green—this will encourage additional chilies to form.

TOP TIPS

Water chili plants regularly, especially in hot weather. Chili plants thrive in the light, so give them plenty to be sure of a fast, strong growth.

Pick chilies regularly to make sure that the plant directs its resources toward producing more of them.

The best color and flavor will come from chilies that are allowed to ripen to a good color, but be aware that leaving chilies on the plant will suppress the production of new ones.

Fresh hot chilies will keep in the refrigerator for one week or in a cool, dry place for up to two weeks.

MONKFISH & BROCCOLINI
COCONUT SOUP

| SERVES: 4 | PREP TIME: 15 mins | COOK TIME: 20 mins |

FISH, COCONUT, AND SPICES WERE SIMPLY MADE FOR EACH OTHER, AS YOU'LL DISCOVER IF YOU TRY THIS QUICK AND SIMPLE SOUP FOR DINNER.

INGREDIENTS

1 large onion, chopped

2 tsp Thai fish sauce

juice of ½ lime

1 red chili, stem removed

1 green chili, stem removed

2 tsp crushed coriander seeds

2 tsp crushed cumin seeds

1-inch piece fresh ginger, chopped

3 garlic cloves, coarsely chopped

½ lemongrass stalk

1½ tbsp peanut oil

5 curry leaves

1¼ cups coconut milk

12 oz broccolini, each spear cut into two pieces

1 lb monkfish fillet, cubed

1 red chili, sliced

1. Add the onion, fish sauce, lime juice, chilies, seeds, ginger, garlic, lemongrass, and half of the oil to the bowl of a blender or food processor and process until you have a paste. Pour the mixture into a skillet and cook over medium heat for 2 minutes. Stir in the curry leaves and coconut milk and simmer for an additional 10 minutes.

2. Meanwhile, add the remaining oil to another skillet and put over high heat. Stir-fry the broccolini for 2 minutes, or until just tender. Set aside.

3. Add the monkfish cubes to the pan with the spices and bring back to a simmer. Cook for 2 minutes, then add the broccolini spears to the pan and continue cooking for an additional minute. Serve the soup with the sliced chili sprinkled over the top.

1 2
3

WHOLE SPICE-CRUSTED RED SNAPPER

SERVES: 2	PREP TIME: 10 mins	COOK TIME: 20 mins

THE SPICES HERE HAVE JUST THE RIGHT AMOUNT OF HEAT AND FLAVOR TO COMPLEMENT THE FISH AND GIVE IT A CRISP CRUST THAT CONTRASTS WITH ITS SOFT MEAT. THE RECIPE IS EASILY SCALED UP IF YOU'RE COOKING FOR MORE THAN TWO PEOPLE. SERVE WITH STEAMED VEGETABLES OR ASPARAGUS.

INGREDIENTS

2 whole red snappers, scaled and gutted

1 lemon, thinly sliced

3½ tsp dukkah spice

⅔ cup ground almonds (almond meal)

¼ cup olive oil

¼ cup fresh cilantro, finely chopped

2 tsp sea salt flakes

grated zest of 1 lemon

1. Preheat the oven to 400°F. Line a large roasting pan with parchment paper and lay the fish on top.

2. Mix the lemon zest, dukkah spice, ground almonds, oil, cilantro, and salt together in a bowl.

3. Spoon 2 tablespoons of the mixture over one side of each fish, pressing it down gently to make a crust. Turn each fish over and spoon 2 tablespoons of the mixture on the other side. Put any remaining mixture in the cavities. Divide the lemon slices between the cavities.

4. Roast for 20 minutes, or until the fish flakes easily when tested with a knife. Let rest for 2 minutes before serving hot.

TIP
WHEN BUYING WHOLE FISH, LOOK FOR BRIGHT AND CLEAR EYES, SHINY SKIN, AND BRIGHT RED GILLS, AND MAKE SURE IT SMELLS FRESH.

CRAWFISH CAKES
WITH MASHED AVOCADO & CHILI

SERVES: 4	PREP TIME: 15 mins, plus 1 hr chilling	COOK TIME: 5–10 mins

TASTY CRAWFISH TAILS ARE A DELIGHTFULLY LOW-FAT TREAT AND, ALTHOUGH THEY DO CONTAIN CHOLESTEROL, THEY CAN BE ENJOYED AS PART OF A BALANCED, HEART-FRIENDLY DIET.

INGREDIENTS

⅔ cup fresh whole wheat bread crumbs

½ tsp pepper

2 tbsp finely chopped fresh flat-leaf parsley

8 oz peeled and cooked crawfish tails, coarsely chopped

¼ cup drained, chopped, and roasted red bell pepper from a jar

1 tsp medium–hot peri-peri sauce

1 tbsp mayonnaise

1 medium egg white, beaten

1 tbsp flour, for dusting

cooking oil spray, for greasing

MASHED AVOCADO & CHILI

1 ripe avocado, peeled, pitted, and sliced

1 small fresh red chili, deseeded and finely chopped

1 scallion, finely chopped

½ tsp smoked paprika

juice of ¼ lime

1. Put the bread crumbs, pepper, and parsley into a bowl and stir well to combine.

2. In a separate bowl, combine the crawfish tails, red bell pepper, peri-peri sauce, and mayonnaise. Stir the bread crumb mixture into the crawfish mixture.

3. Add the beaten egg white and mix to a moderately firm mixture; the cakes will be firm once they are cooked. Divide and shape into four round cakes and sprinkle with flour. If you have time, chill for up to 1 hour.

4. To make the mashed avocado, put the avocado slices into a bowl and coarsely mash with a fork. Stir in the chili, scallion, paprika, and lime juice.

5. Spray a nonstick skillet with the cooking oil and put over medium–high heat. Add the crawfish cakes and cook for 2–3 minutes, or until the underside is crisp and golden. Turn and cook for an additional 2–3 minutes, or until cooked through. Serve the cakes immediately with the mashed avocado on top.

1 2
4

FISH WITH CHILI, WHITE WINE & TAPENADE

SERVES: 4	PREP TIME: 5 mins	COOK TIME: 15 mins

THIS FISH, CHILI, AND TAPENADE DISH IS A BREEZE TO PREPARE, AND YET IT ALSO DELIVERS SOME SOPHISTICATED FLAVORS.

INGREDIENTS
1 tbsp olive oil

4 white fish fillets

¼ cup tapenade

1 small red finger chili, deseeded and chopped

¼ cup freshly grated Parmesan cheese

¼ cup dry white wine

salt and pepper (optional)

3½ cups cooked rice, to serve

1. Preheat the oven to 425°F. Brush a wide, ovenproof dish with the oil.

2. Season the fish with salt and pepper, if using, and place in the prepared dish in a single layer.

3. Mix the tapenade and chili together and spread over the fish, then sprinkle with the cheese.

4. Pour the wine around the fish and bake in the preheated oven for about 15 minutes, or until the flesh flakes easily. Serve with the rice.

SEARED SCALLOPS
WITH FRESH MINT
& RED CHILI DRESSING

SERVES: 4–6	PREP TIME: 35 mins	COOK TIME: 25–28 mins

ENJOY THESE SEARED SCALLOPS ON A BED OF PEPPERY GREENS, WITH HERBED LENTILS, PAN-FRIED PANCETTA, AND A DRIZZLE OF MINT-CHILI DRESSING.

INGREDIENTS
½ cup French green lentils

2 garlic cloves

1 celery stalk

2 bay leaves

20 fresh parsley leaves, with stems

olive oil, for drizzling and frying

zest and juice of 1 lemon

2 tbsp aged red wine vinegar

20 fresh basil leaves, coarsely chopped

20 fresh mint leaves, coarsely chopped

handful of arugula leaves, coarsely chopped

20 scallops

8 slices pancetta

salt and pepper (optional)

arugula, to serve

MINT & RED CHILI DRESSING
2 red chilies, deseeded and chopped

small bunch of fresh mint, finely chopped

½ cup extra virgin olive oil

juice of 1 lemon

salt and pepper (optional)

1. Cover the lentils with water in a large saucepan and add the garlic, celery stalk, bay leaves, and a few parsley stems. Bring to a boil, then reduce to a simmer.

2. Cook the lentils for 12–15 minutes, until they are al dente and nutty. Remove from the heat and drain off most of the water. Remove the garlic, bay leaves, celery stalk, and parsley stems. Season the lentils with olive oil, lemon zest and juice, some of the vinegar, and salt and pepper, if using.

3. When the lentils have cooled slightly, add the herbs and arugula and stir until combined. Set the lentils aside.

4. For the dressing, mix together the chilies and mint in a bowl with the olive oil and lemon juice, and season with salt and pepper, if using.

5. Clean the scallops by removing the small opaque muscle from the sides, and dry them on paper towels. Add a tablespoon of oil to a skillet over high heat, add the pancetta and cook the slices for 2 minutes on each side, until crispy. Drain on paper towels.

6. Keep the skillet over high heat. Pat the scallops until dry. Add a splash more olive oil to the skillet. Add the scallops and cook for 45 seconds. Use a metal spatula to quickly and gently flip the scallops. Cook on the second side for about 40 seconds; when the scallops are caramelized on both sides, remove and place on clean paper towels.

7. Add a splash of vinegar to deglaze the skillet, then add the liquid to the dressing. To serve, sprinkle the herbed lentils over the arugula, and arrange the scallops and the pancetta on top. Spoon some mint and chili dressing on top and serve immediately.

BAKED FISH
WRAPPED IN
BANANA LEAVES

| SERVES: 4 | PREP TIME: 15–20 mins | COOK TIME: 15–20 mins |

THIS DELICIOUS INDIAN BAKED FISH DISH LOOKS PRETTY SERVED WRAPPED IN BANANA LEAVES. YOUR GUESTS WILL ENJOY THE MOUTHWATERING AROMAS THAT ARE RELEASED AS THEY UNWRAP THEIR INDIVIDUAL PACKAGES AT THE TABLE.

INGREDIENTS

4 (7 oz) thick cod fillets, skinned

2 tsp ground turmeric

1 large fresh banana leaf

SPICE PASTE

2 tsp ground cumin

2 tsp ground coriander

1½ tsp palm sugar or brown sugar

1 cup coconut cream

4 fresh red chilies, deseeded and chopped

2½ cups chopped fresh cilantro

¼ cup chopped fresh mint

5 garlic cloves, chopped

1 tsp finely grated fresh ginger

¼ cup vegetable oil or peanut oil

juice of 2 limes

2 tsp salt

1. Preheat the oven to 400°F.

2. Place the fish fillets in a single layer on a plate and sprinkle with the turmeric. Rub into the fish and set aside.

3. Put the ingredients for the spice paste into a food processor and blend until fairly smooth.

4. Cut the banana leaf into four 9½-inch squares. Soften the banana leaf squares by dipping them into a saucepan of hot water for a few seconds. Once the banana leaf squares have become pliant, wipe them dry with paper towels and arrange on a work surface.

5. Apply the spice paste liberally to both sides of each piece of fish. Place a piece of fish on top of each banana leaf square and wrap up like a package, securing with bamboo skewers or twine.

6. Place the packages on a baking pan and bake in the preheated oven for 15–20 minutes, until cooked through. Transfer to plates and serve immediately.

BAKING, DESSERTS & DRINKS

Sweet and spicy flavors can complement one another surprisingly well, as you'll discover with this irresistible selection of spice-infused cakes, desserts, and drinks. Go ahead and indulge in smooth Chocolate Mousse with a Chili Kick; Spicy Squash Cake; Carrot, Fruit & Cardamom Rolls; or knock your socks off with a Chili & Wasabi Bloody Mary.

CHOCOLATE MOUSSE WITH A CHILI KICK

| SERVES: 4 | PREP TIME: 20 mins, plus 2 hrs chilling | COOK TIME: 5 mins |

CHOCOLATE AND CHILI MIGHT NOT FEEL LIKE A NATURAL PAIRING, BUT THEY WORK TOGETHER WONDERFULLY—A SUBTLE NOTE OF CHILI BRINGS A DELIGHTFUL WARMTH TO THIS SMOOTH CHOCOLATE MOUSSE.

INGREDIENTS

6 oz bittersweet chocolate, broken into pieces

pinch of salt

4 extra-large eggs, separated

¼ cup superfine sugar

⅔ cup heavy cream

1 tsp chipotle powder

2 tsp orange zest

⅔ cup sour cherries

½ cup dark rum

½ cup roasted hazelnuts

1. Put the chocolate pieces into a large heatproof bowl set over a saucepan of gently simmering water and heat, stirring occasionally, until melted. Remove from the heat and set aside to cool.

2. Once the chocolate has cooled, beat in the salt, egg yolks, and sugar.

3. In a separate bowl whisk the heavy cream until it thickens slightly.

4. In a clean bowl whisk the egg whites until stiff peaks form.

5. Add the chipotle powder and 1 teaspoon of the orange zest to the chocolate mixture, then fold in the cream, followed by the egg whites. Divide among four glasses and place in the refrigerator for 2 hours to set.

6. Meanwhile, soak the sour cherries in the rum and coarsely chop the hazelnuts.

7. Just before serving remove the mousse from the refrigerator and top with the rum-soaked sour cherries, hazelnuts, and remaining orange zest.

CINNAMON-SPICED SYLLABUB

| SERVES: 8 | PREP TIME: 10 mins, plus at least 1 hr chilling | COOK TIME: none |

WONDERFULLY EASY TO MAKE, THESE LITTLE CLOUDS OF LIGHTLY WHIPPED CREAM WILL LOOK BEAUTIFUL PRESENTED IN YOUR PRETTIEST GLASSES. YOUR GUESTS WILL LOVE THEIR MIDDLE-EASTERN SCENT OF CINNAMON AND ORANGE FLOWER WATER.

INGREDIENTS

juice of 2 lemons

½ tsp ground cinnamon, plus a pinch to decorate

1 tsp orange flower water

½ cup superfine sugar

2½ cups heavy cream

1 tbsp chopped pistachios, to decorate

2 tbsp pomegranate arils, to decorate

1. Put the lemon juice, cinnamon, orange flower water, and sugar into a large bowl and whisk briefly to dissolve the sugar. Add the cream and lightly whisk until it just comes together as barely solid—this should take no more than 1 minute.

2. Spoon the syllabub into eight small ½-cup glasses. Sprinkle with the remaining cinnamon, pistachios, and pomegranate arils. Cover and chill in the refrigerator for at least 1 hour or up to a day. Serve cold.

TIP
SYLLABUB SHOULD NOT BE THE TEXTURE OF WHIPPED CREAM, SO BE CAREFUL NOT TO OVERWHISK IT AFTER ADDING THE CREAM.

APRICOTS POACHED IN ROSEWATER & CARDAMOM WITH GINGER YOGURT

SERVES: 4	PREP TIME: 20 mins	COOK TIME: 15 mins

THIS IS ONE OF THE EASIEST DESSERTS TO MAKE, AND THE APRICOTS WILL BRING SOME SUNSHINE TO THE TABLE. YOUR GUESTS WILL BE DELIGHTED BY ITS EXOTIC FRAGRANCE AND GENTLY SPICED FLAVOR.

INGREDIENTS
¾ cup superfine sugar

6 green cardamom pods, lightly crushed

1 cinnamon stick

¼ tsp rosewater

1½ cups water

4 apricots, halved and pitted

1 tbsp dried edible rose petals, to decorate (optional)

GINGER YOGURT
½ cup plain Greek yogurt

1-inch piece of fresh ginger, peeled and finely grated

1. Put the sugar, cardamom, cinnamon, rosewater, and water into a saucepan. Stir and cook over low heat until the sugar has dissolved.

2. Increase the heat to medium–high, bring to a boil, then lower in the apricots using a slotted spoon. Reduce the heat to low and simmer for 5 minutes. Turn off the heat and let them stand in the syrup for 10 minutes.

3. Transfer the apricots to a serving bowl using the slotted spoon. When cool enough to handle, slip off and discard the skins.

4. For the ginger yogurt, put the yogurt in a small serving bowl, stir in the ginger, cover, and set aside.

5. Return the syrup to the heat and boil until reduced by half. Pour the syrup over the apricots, then sprinkle with the dried rose petals, if using. Serve the apricots with the ginger yogurt. If not serving immediately, let cool, then cover and chill in the refrigerator and serve cold.

TIP
ROSEWATER COMES IN DIFFERENT STRENGTHS, DEPENDING ON THE MAKER. ADJUST ACCORDING TO YOUR BRAND AND TASTE.

INDIAN
RICE DESSERT

| SERVES: 4 | PREP TIME: 20–25 mins, plus chilling | COOK TIME: 30–35 mins |

FOR THIS DISH, RICE FLOUR IS COOKED IN THICKENED MILK WITH APRICOTS, RAISINS, ALMONDS, AND PISTACHIOS, WITH THE EXOTIC AROMA OF ROSEWATER AND CARDAMOM. IT IS BEST SERVED CHILLED.

INGREDIENTS

pinch of saffron, pounded

2 tbsp hot milk

3 tbsp clarified butter or unsalted butter

⅓ cup rice flour

¼ cup slivered almonds

3 tbsp seedless raisins

2½ cups whole milk

2 cups evaporated milk

¼ cup superfine sugar

12 dried apricots, sliced

1 tsp freshly ground cardamom seeds

½ tsp freshly grated nutmeg

2 tbsp rosewater

TO GARNISH

¼ cup walnut pieces

2 tbsp shelled unsalted pistachios

1. Put the pounded saffron into the hot milk and soak until needed.

2. Reserve 2 teaspoons of the butter and melt the rest in a heavy saucepan over low heat. Add the rice flour, almonds, and raisins and cook, stirring, for 2 minutes. Add the whole milk, increase the heat to medium, and cook, stirring, until it begins to bubble gently. Reduce the heat to low and cook, stirring frequently, for 10–12 minutes, to prevent the mixture from sticking to the bottom of the pan.

3. Add the evaporated milk, sugar, and apricots, reserving a few slices to decorate. Cook, stirring, until the mixture thickens but can still be poured.

4. Add the cardamom, nutmeg, and rosewater, stir to distribute well, and remove from the heat. Let cool, then cover and chill in the refrigerator for at least 2 hours.

5. Melt the reserved butter in a small saucepan over low heat. Add the walnuts and cook, stirring, until they brown slightly. Remove and drain on paper towels. Brown the pistachios in the remaining butter in the saucepan, remove, and drain on paper towels. Let the pistachios cool, then lightly crush.

6. Serve the dessert garnished with the fried nuts and the reserved apricot slices.

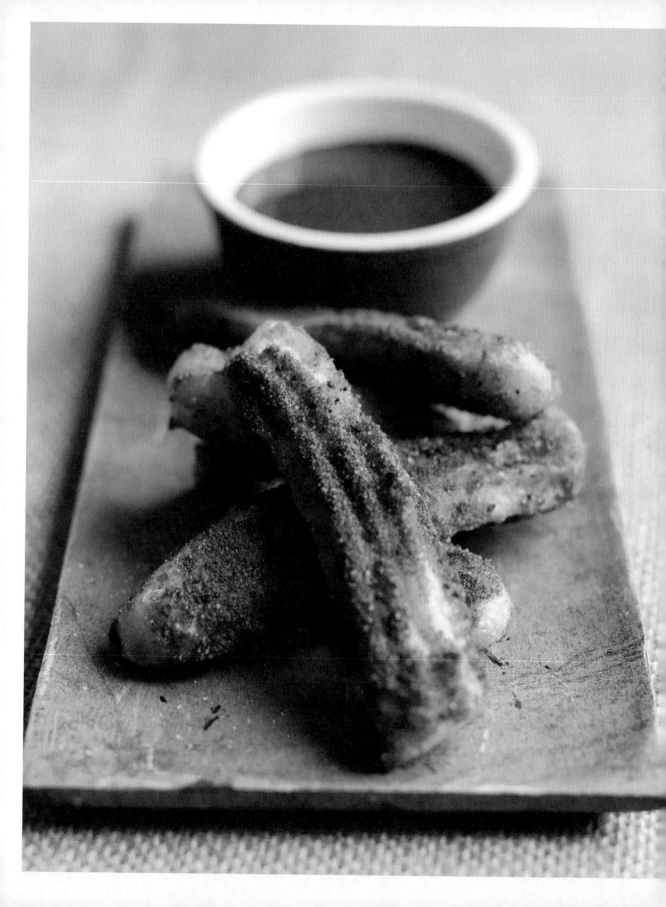

CHILI & CHOCOLATE CHURROS

| **MAKES:** 16 | **PREP TIME:** 35 mins, plus cooling | **COOK TIME:** 30–35 mins |

CHURROS ARE FRIED-DOUGH SNACKS. IN THIS YUMMY VERSION, SEMISWEET
CHOCOLATE, COCOA, CHILI, AND CREAM DO THEM PROUD.

INGREDIENTS

1 stick unsalted butter, diced

1 cup water

1¼ cups all-purpose flour, sifted

large pinch of salt

2 extra-large eggs, beaten

½ small red chili,
deseeded and minced

oil, for deep-frying

¼ cup sugar

2 tsp unsweetened cocoa
powder, sifted

CHOCOLATE SAUCE

3 oz semisweet chocolate,
broken into pieces

½ cup heavy cream

½ tsp vanilla extract

1 tsp crushed red pepper flakes

1. To make the chocolate sauce, put the chocolate and cream in a heatproof bowl set over a saucepan of gently simmering water, and heat until the chocolate is melted. Remove from the heat and stir until smooth, then stir in the vanilla extract and red pepper flakes. Set aside and keep warm.

2. Put the butter and water into a large saucepan over low heat and heat until the butter has melted. Bring to a boil, remove from the heat, and add the flour and salt. Beat thoroughly until the mixture is smooth and comes away from the side of the pan. Let cool for 5 minutes, then gradually beat in the eggs to make a thick and glossy paste. Beat in the chili.

3. Heat enough oil for deep-frying in a large saucepan or deep fryer to 350–375°F, or until a cube of bread browns in 30 seconds. Spoon the paste into a large pastry bag fitted with a large star tip and pipe four 4-inch lengths of the paste into the hot oil. Fry for 2–3 minutes, turning frequently, until crisp and golden. Remove with a slotted spoon and drain on paper towels. Keep warm while frying the remaining mixture.

4. Mix together the sugar and cocoa powder on a flat plate and toss the warm churros in the mixture to coat. Serve immediately with the chocolate sauce for dipping.

SPICES FROM BARKS, FLOWER BUDS & ROOTS

Spices can be sourced from arils, barks, dried flower buds, stigmas, and roots, or from dried fruits or seeds. Here are a selection that fall into the first category, as well as some mixed spice combinations.

Cinnamon (see opposite, top left) is obtained from the inner bark of the Cinnamomum tree, which is native to Sri Lanka. The bark is dried and rolled up to make the long, slender tubes that characterize this spice. Cinnamon is also sold as a powder and is used in both savory and sweet dishes.

Cloves (see opposite, bottom right) are the aromatic dried red flower buds of Syzygium aromaticum, an evergreen tree from eastern Indonesia. They have a hard surrounding and contain an oily compound that creates the distinctive warm, sweet, aromatic taste. Cloves are used to give aromatic qualities to hot drinks and are often used in spice blends.

Coriander, known as cilantro in its leaf form, is used for its leaves and seeds. The leaves have a subtle citrus quality whereas the dried coriander seeds, of which there are two in each fruit, have a much stronger lemony flavor and bring warm, spicy overtones. Ground coriander is used as a key feature of various spice mixtures, such as garam masala and harissa.

Curry powder is a premixed combination of spices, usually chili powder, turmeric, coriander, cumin, ginger, and pepper. Strengths can vary from mild to strong. It it believed to have been created by the British to recreate the depth of flavor in Indian spice dishes, although spice mixtures are also common throughout Asia.

Ginger is a hot, fragrant spice obtained from the rhizome of the ginger plant Zingiber officinale. The bulbous roots are widely used in southern Asian cuisines for beverages, soups, sauces, and baking. It is available fresh or ground and can be used in sweet and savory dishes.

Mace is obtained from the aril of the nutmeg plant, Myristica fragrans—the aril is the dried reddish covering of the nutmeg seed. The flavor, although similar to nutmeg, is lighter and sweeter and it has a more intense aroma.

Saffron is a spice from the flower stigma of the saffron crocus, Crocus sativus (see opposite, top right), which is native to southwest Asia. The flowers each have three vivid crimson stigmas, and it is from these that the threads are collected and dried. It is available in bright-red threads, which carry a musty, floral aroma and flavor. Labor-intensive to produce, saffron is one of the more expensive spices.

Turmeric (see opposite, bottom left) comes from the root of Curcuma longa and has a peppery, bitter flavor with orange and ginger overtones. It is used in mustard, which gives it its bright yellow shade.

Za'atar is the name of a herb, but also of a spice mixture made from a combination of dried herbs, spices, and seeds, such as sesame seeds, dried sumac, and salt. Za'atar is widely used in Middle Eastern cooking.

SPICY SQUASH CAKE

SERVES: 8	PREP TIME: 35–40 mins	COOK TIME: 1¼ hrs

BUTTERNUT SQUASH ADDS A RICH TEXTURE AND DEPTH TO SWEET CAKES AND MAKES A WONDERFUL COMPLEMENT TO DRIED FRUIT AND WARMING SPICES.

INGREDIENTS

⅓ cup golden raisins

2 tsp unsalted butter, for greasing

2 cups peeled, deseeded, and diced butternut squash

1¼ sticks plus 1 tbsp unsalted butter

¾ cup superfine or granulated sugar

½ cup chopped almonds

¼ cup Italian candied peel

finely grated zest of 1 lemon

1½ tsp ground cinnamon

1½ tsp ground ginger

¾ cup Kamut flour

1 heaping tsp baking powder

2 eggs, separated

1 tbsp confectioners' sugar, for dusting

1. Put the golden raisins into a bowl, pour over enough boiling water to cover, and let soak.

2. Preheat the oven to 350°F. Grease and line a 9-inch round springform cake pan.

3. Put the squash and butter into a saucepan. Cover and cook over medium heat for about 15 minutes, until soft. Transfer to a bowl and beat until smooth.

4. Stir in the sugar, almonds, candied peel, lemon zest, cinnamon, ginger, and drained golden raisins, and mix well to combine.

5. Sift together the flour and baking powder. Gradually beat into the squash mixture.

6. Beat the egg yolks for about 3 minutes, until thick. Fold into the squash mixture.

7. Whisk the egg whites until they hold stiff peaks. Fold carefully into the mixture using a large metal spoon. Spoon the batter into the prepared pan.

8. Bake in the preheated oven for 1 hour, or until a toothpick inserted into the center comes out clean. Turn out onto a wire rack to cool. Dust with the confectioners' sugar just before serving.

3 4
7

CARROT, FRUIT & CARDAMOM ROLLS

MAKES: 16	**PREP TIME:** 50–55 mins, plus 2–2½ hrs rising	**COOK TIME:** 30–35 mins

THE CARROT TAKES CENTER STAGE IN THESE DELICIOUS SCANDINAVIAN-STYLE ROLLS. BURSTING WITH CANDIED FRUIT AND LIGHTLY SPICED WITH CARDAMOM, THEY ARE HEAVENLY WHEN EATEN FRESHLY BAKED.

INGREDIENTS

1 cup sliced carrots

2¾ cups white bread flour, sifted

2 tbsp active dry yeast

3 tbsp superfine sugar

2 tsp ground cardamom seeds (from about 24 pods)

½ tsp salt

1 stick unsalted butter

1 egg, lightly beaten

⅓ cup lukewarm milk

1 tbsp flour, for dusting

1 tbsp oil, for oiling

⅔ cup chopped candied fruit

1 egg yolk

1 tbsp cold milk

1 tbsp confectioners' sugar, for sprinkling

1. Put the carrots into the top of a steamer and steam for 15 minutes, until tender, then blend to a paste in a blender. Set aside until needed.

2. Line a baking pan with a silicone sheet. Put the flour, yeast, superfine sugar, cardamom, and salt into a large bowl and mix to combine. Melt all but 2 tablespoons of the butter and let cool slightly. Mix the beaten egg with the lukewarm milk and the melted butter. Stir into the flour mixture, then add the carrot paste. Mix to a soft dough.

3. Turn out the dough onto a floured board and knead for 10–15 minutes, until silky. Transfer to a lightly oiled bowl, cover with plastic wrap, and let stand in a warm place for 1½–2 hours, or until doubled in size. Turn out onto a floured board and punch down to get rid of the air. Roll out thinly to a 18 x 12-inch rectangle.

4. Melt the remaining butter and brush it over the dough surface. Sprinkle with the candied fruit, taking it to the edge of the dough and breaking up any clumps.

5. Roll the dough from the long edge into a log. Slice into 1-inch circles and place on the prepared baking pan. Cover with plastic wrap and let rise for 30 minutes. Meanwhile, preheat the oven to 400°F.

6. Mix the egg yolk with the cold milk and brush over the rolls, then bake in the preheated oven for 10–15 minutes, until golden.

7. Transfer to a wire rack to cool, then sprinkle with the confectioners' sugar. The rolls are best eaten fresh from the oven.

CHOCOLATE PECAN BROWNIES WITH CHILI

MAKES: 12	PREP TIME: 30 mins	COOK TIME: 20–25 mins

HOW ABOUT SOME DECADENT STICKY, CHEWY BROWNIES WITH A TWIST? THE CHILI FLAVORING IN THESE IS SUBTLE ENOUGH TO WAKE UP THE TASTE BUDS WITHOUT SHOCKING THE PALATE.

INGREDIENTS

3½ tbsp unsalted butter, softened, plus extra for greasing

½ cup granulated sugar

3 eggs, beaten

¾ cup all-purpose flour

¾ tsp baking powder

1 cup unsweetened cocoa powder

1 tsp crushed red pepper flakes

about 1 tbsp rum

1 cup pecan halves

1. Preheat the oven to 350°F. Grease an 8-inch square or equivalent-size rectangular shallow baking pan.

2. Using a wooden spoon, beat the butter with sugar in a warm bowl until pale and fluffy. Alternatively, process in a food processor. Beat in the eggs, a little at a time, adding a little flour if the mixture begins to curdle. Switching to a metal spoon, gently fold in the flour, baking powder, cocoa powder, and red pepper flakes. Stir in the rum and add enough water until you have a cake batter that drops easily from the spoon. Taste and see if you need to add a little more chili. Fold in the pecans, reserving a few of the best for the top.

3. Pour the batter into the prepared pan, smoothing it into the corners. Sprinkle the top with the reserved pecans.

4. Bake in the preheated oven for 20–25 minutes, or until crusted on top but still not quite set. Remove from the oven and cut into 12 squares while still warm.

SPICED PUMPKIN
TARTS

| SERVES: 4 | PREP TIME: 30 mins, plus cooling | COOK TIME: 40 mins |

THESE MINI TARTS HAVE ALL THE FLAVOR OF TRADITIONAL PUMPKIN PIE. THEY'RE SIMPLY DELICIOUS SERVED WITH COFFEE OR AS AN INDULGENT DESSERT WITH WHIPPED CREAM OR VANILLA ICE CREAM.

INGREDIENTS

2 tsp butter, for greasing

3½ cups pumpkin or butternut squash, cut into ½-inch pieces

2 tsp butter

1 tbsp maple syrup

1 piece preserved ginger in syrup, finely chopped

¼ tsp cinnamon

¼ tsp allspice

6 sheets of phyllo pastry

2 tbsp canola oil, for brushing

1 tbsp confectioners' sugar, for dusting

1. Preheat the oven to 375°F. Lightly grease four 4-inch tart pans.

2. Put the pumpkin or squash on a baking sheet and dot with the butter. Roast in the preheated oven for 5 minutes, then stir and return to the oven for an additional 20 minutes, or until the pumpkin is beginning to brown.

3. Stir the maple syrup, ginger, cinnamon, and allspice into the pumpkin and cook for an additional 5 minutes. Let cool.

4. Cut the pastry into twelve 4-inch squares. Brush four of the squares with oil. Place a second sheet of pastry on top of each, at an angle to the first so that the points of the squares do not align—you are aiming to create a star shape. Brush with oil again and repeat with the remaining pastry sheets to make four stacks, each with three layers.

5. Transfer the pastry stacks into the prepared pans, press down gently, and bake in the preheated oven for 8–10 minutes, or until crisp and golden.

6. Fill the pastry shells with the pumpkin mixture. Dust the tarts with the confectioners' sugar and serve immediately.

CHILI & AMARANTH
CORN BREAD

MAKES: 1 loaf	**PREP TIME:** 20 mins	**COOK TIME:** 55 mins, plus cooling

THE COMBINATION OF CORN AND CHILI BRINGS A NEW DYNAMIC TO CORN BREAD. IT CAN BE SERVED IN MANY WAYS, SUCH AS WITH SOUP, STEW, OR CHILI, WITH DEEP-FRIED CHICKEN, OR SIMPLY PAIRED WITH A FRESH SALAD.

INGREDIENTS

2–3 fresh red chilies, or to taste

¾ cup amaranth flour

¾ cup all-purpose white flour

¾ cup cornmeal

1 tbsp baking powder

1 tsp baking soda

1½ tsp salt

¼ cup granulated sugar

1 cup shredded cheddar cheese

3 eggs

1 cup buttermilk

5 tbsp butter, melted and cooled slightly, plus extra for greasing

⅓ cup fresh or frozen corn, thawed if frozen

1. Preheat the oven to 400°F. Preheat the broiler and grease a 9 x 5-inch loaf pan.

2. Put the chilies under the preheated broiler and cook, turning occasionally, for 5–7 minutes, until blackened all over. Remove the skins and seeds and finely chop the flesh.

3. Sift together the amaranth flour, white flour, cornmeal, baking powder, baking soda, and salt into a large bowl. Stir in the sugar and cheese.

4. Whisk the eggs with the buttermilk and melted butter until well blended.

5. Make a well in the center of the flour mixture and pour in the egg mixture. Mix together with a fork, gradually drawing in the dry ingredients from the side.

6. Stir in the chilies and corn and spoon the batter into the prepared pan, leveling the surface. Bake in the preheated oven for 40–45 minutes, until a toothpick inserted into the center comes out clean.

7. Let cool in the pan for 10 minutes, then turn out onto a wire rack and let cool completely.

LIME & CHILI
SORBET ICE POPS

| MAKES: 8 | PREP TIME: 15 mins, plus cooling and freezing | COOK TIME: 10 mins |

THESE PALE, CHILI-SPECKLED SORBET STICKS ARE A TWIST ON THE CLASSIC LEMON SORBET—THEY HAVE A HIDDEN KICK FROM THE CHILI. FOR A LESS SPICY VERSION, REDUCE THE AMOUNT OF CHILI.

INGREDIENTS
½ cup superfine sugar

1 red chili, deseeded and minced

1¾ cups water

4 large limes

8 thin slices from a small lime

1. Put the sugar, chili, and water into a saucepan. Place over medium–low heat, stirring, for 6–8 minutes, or until the sugar has dissolved. Increase the heat to medium–high and bring the mixture to a boil, then remove from the heat.

2. Finely grate the zest of two of the limes into the mixture and stir. Cover and let cool completely; this will take about 1 hour.

3. Squeeze the juice from the four limes and stir it into the mixture.

4. Pour the mixture into eight ¼-cup ice pop molds and place a lime slice into each mold. Insert the ice pop sticks and freeze for 5–6 hours, or until firm.

5. To unmold the ice pops, dip the frozen molds into warm water for a few seconds, and gently release the pops while holding the sticks.

CHILI & WASABI
BLOODY MARY

| SERVES: 1 | PREP TIME: 20 mins | COOK TIME: none |

THIS ZINGY COCKTAIL OFFERS NO HALF MEASURES IN TERMS OF ITS HEAT. SAVORY COCKTAILS ARE THE NEW TREND, AND THIS VERSION OF BLOODY MARY, WITH CHILI POWDER, LIME JUICE, WASABI, AND BULLDOG SAUCE, WILL HIT THE SPOT.

INGREDIENTS
¾ oz vodka

¾ oz sake

½ oz lime juice

½ tsp Korean chili powder

¼ tsp garlic powder

1-inch piece fresh ginger, grated

1 tsp Thai fish sauce

½ tsp wasabi paste

2 tsp tonkatsu bulldog sauce
or other hot sauce

whole ice cubes

¾ cup tomato juice

daikon radish stick, to garnish

1. Mix together the vodka, sake, lime juice, chili powder, garlic powder, ginger, fish sauce, wasabi paste, and bulldog sauce in a Collins or highball glass using a barspoon.

2. Stir well, making sure all the ingredients are combined.

3. Add a few ice cubes and the tomato juice and stir again.

4. Garnish with the daikon radish and serve immediately.

TIP
THIS IS A DELIGHT WHEN SERVED WITH OYSTERS—AND YOU CAN ADJUST THE SEASONINGS TO TASTE.

VEGETABLE TUMMY TREAT

| SERVES: 1 | PREP TIME: 15 mins | COOK TIME: none |

WAKE UP YOUR BODY AND STIMULATE YOUR DIGESTIVE SYSTEM WITH THIS FRESH-TASTING ORANGE AND TOMATO DRINK. THERE IS ALSO A KICK IN THE TAIL DELIVERED BY THE CHILI TO SHAKE UP THOSE TASTE BUDS.

INGREDIENTS

3 oranges, zest and a little pith removed

1 carrot, halved

2 tomatoes, coarsely chopped

½ cup chilled water

1 small green chili, halved

2 celery stalks, thickly sliced

2 tsp hemp seed oil

1. Cut two oranges in half and feed them and the carrot through a juicer. Pour the juice into a blender. Coarsely chop and deseed the remaining orange, then put it, the tomatoes, and water into the blender and blend until smooth. Add the chili and celery and blend again. Pour into a glass, stir in the hemp seed oil, and serve.

INDEX